Stephen Alexander Hodgman

The nation's sin and punishment

The hand of God visible in the overthrow of slavery

Stephen Alexander Hodgman

The nation's sin and punishment
The hand of God visible in the overthrow of slavery

ISBN/EAN: 9783744722643

Printed in Europe, USA, Canada, Australia, Japan

Cover: Foto ©ninafisch / pixelio.de

More available books at **www.hansebooks.com**

THE NATION'S

SIN AND PUNISHMENT;

OR,

THE HAND OF GOD

VISIBLE IN THE

OVERTHROW OF SLAVERY.

BY A CHAPLAIN OF THE U. S. ARMY,

Who has been, thirty years, a resident of the Slave States.

NEW YORK:
M. DOOLADY, Agent, 49 WALKER ST.
AMERICAN NEWS COMPANY, 121 NASSAU STREET.
R. CRAIGHEAD, Printer.
1864.

Stereotyped by VINCENT DILL,
No. 24 Beekman St., N. Y.

J. Frank.

CONTENTS.

DEDICATION.

To the Christian people of this great and free land, this little volume is affectionately dedicated. We have not, as we should have done, recognized the hand of our God, in the terrible judgments that have come on our Nation. The design of this little volume is, to trace those judgments to their legitimate and just cause, and to view, in its religious aspect, the sanguinary strife, through which we are now passing. As a Nation, we are *guilty*, in having tolerated and upheld for a long series of years, the most matured system of iniquity and oppression, that devils or wicked men ever yet devised. The wonder is, that, the Divine judgments did not descend upon us long ago. But our eyes have been opened at length, and we are thankful, that our land is to be cleansed from its pollutions.

THE AUTHOR.

In Camp, November, 1863.

THE AUTHOR'S INTRODUCTION.

THE writer of this fugitive Essay, has no apology to make, for this Introduction of himself to the Public, but he deems it proper to remark, that, having received a Northern birth and education, he has spent the last thirty-two years of his life in the Slave States. He thinks, therefore, that he can say, without the charge of vanity, he feels competent, from his own *personal knowledge*, to give, correctly, the characteristics of Slavery, and of Slave-holders. He would also further remark, that he is not now, and that he never has been an *Abolitionist*, of the radical school. He has always been an anti-slavery man. But from the very hour when the Rebels opened their batteries on Fort Sumter, he has been an earnest and practi-

cal *Emancipationist;* for he then became
assured that the downfall of slavery had
been decreed of Heaven, and he knew that
it would be only madness to be found in opposition to the WILL OF GOD, as revealed in
the terrible dispensations of his Providence.
He had always endeavored to stand, on *conservative* ground, acting in the spirit of conciliation and compromise, in which spirit the
nation had grown up as a unity, and had
advanced to a degree of unexampled prosperity. He belonged to that branch of the
Church, which entirely ignored the right of
Ecclesiastical bodies, to *legislate* on the subject of slavery. His motive, as well as that
of the brethren of the same Church, who
acted in this *conservative* spirit, was to prevent, if possible, the dismemberment of the
Church, and the dissolution of the States'
Union.

But we have been disappointed. Our policy was wrong. This confession does not
imply that we had adopted a wrong policy,

intentionally, to accomplish a laudable purpose. The Union has been dissolved, to be reconstructed, we doubt not, on a better, and surer foundation. The Church has been rent asunder, notwithstanding all our conservatism. Slavery has done the mischief. Conservatism could not prevent it. We were only mistaken as to what the Almighty had willed. The Abolitionists were but instruments who had a special agency to perform in the work. But no thanks to them! the war had become necessary. A wise and just Providence has directed all the steps. The writer exults in the belief, that the revolution will be most glorious, in its results, to the Nation at large, and to the interests of the universal Church Militant.

I.

WARS—JUST OR UNJUST.

I HAVE somewhere read, in history, of two brothers, who quarreled for the possession of a throne. The contest became so fierce, that each decided to raise an army, and to settle their claims on the field of blood. When the combat was over, the two brothers were found, side by side, in the embrace of death. Their mutual animosity had been so violent, that they had sought and encountered one another, in single combat, and had fallen, on the same spot, each pierced by the other's sword. This was a war between two brothers.

The war now desolating this once prosperous and happy country, is *a war between brothers!*

Tell me, O ye people of America, who boast of your christianity, how, think you, a Holy God must look down, from his glorious habitation, on such a strife between brothers! How must the blessed and holy angels view such a contest as this! With what sentiments must every truly devout and Christian philanthropist throughout the world, regard this grand display of rage and hellish passions! Can it be imagined, that pure and holy beings, either in heaven or upon earth, can look on such a contest with emotions of satisfaction or complacency? Does the exhibition of such demoniacal wrath, indicate that man was, originally, endowed with reason and a moral conscience? that the image of Deity was instamped on his heart? and that he was made, in form and soul, erect, and superior to savage beasts whose nature thirsts for blood?

The existence of war proves that man is a fallen being. He fell from his allegiance to a Holy God. This is the reason, and no other can be assigned, why he is ever made willing to imbrue his hand in the blood of his brother man. If it were not so, this earth would never have become the theater of wars, and deadly strifes; but the whole family of Adam had remained united together, in the bonds of love and a sacred brotherhood.

What a terrible thing sin is! It sowed the first seeds of discord! It first caused the tocsin of war to be sounded in the peaceful realms of the new and green earth, which God created and designed as the abode of man! It has strewn every battle-field with the dead and mangled corpses of earth's children!

What a frightful thing sin is! No wonder a Holy God hates sin, with an infinite and eternal hatred!

View war, in its inception and in its progress —what are its paraphernalia, and its accompaniments? Human ingenuity has been taxed to the utmost extent—science has been laid under contribution, to furnish the most deadly and destructive implements of death that could be invented.

See the opposing hosts drawn up in battle array; they are members of the same common family of God, who have fallen out with one another, and are met to settle the controversy. The weapons of death gleam in their hands. The passions of hell rage and burn in their hearts. The trumpet sounds! Wild and savage yells are heard! It is the signal for the commencement of the slaughter—the battle begins! There is a deafening roar of artillery—the plains are enveloped in clouds of smoke—the ground is strewn with the dead—the air is rent with the groans of the dying! This is war! aye, this is honorable and christian warfare! And this is the mode in which brethren choose to settle the differences that arise between them! Can a righteous God approve of such horrible carnage?

It has been represented that war is a *necessary evil*. It is so, only to the extent that sin abounds —for every war is the effect of sin.

Defensive wars are justifiable. The present civil-war, as undertaken to defend and maintain the Government of the country, and to perpetuate the glorious inheritance of civil and religious liberty, bequeathed to us by our ancestors, is a necessary, and, therefore, a just war. But, as undertaken by the Rebels, to break up the Government, it is not a just war, but a horrible revolt against God, and against human rights. There was no imperative and absolute necessity, that forced them to engage in this war. They did it voluntarily, and without a just cause. Therefore, there is no palliation for their guilt, and the vengeance of a just God, is inflicted, and must be inflicted on them.

Notwithstanding that all wars are the result of sin, yet, as I have already intimated, some wars are just and necessary. And, it may be said, that, as permitted by the Supreme Being, all wars result in good to the human family. We cannot always tell what good, but sometimes we can.

We are sure that the war of our Independence, which laid the foundations of the greatest nation, and the best government on earth, effected an amount of good which it is scarcely possible for the human intellect to estimate.

The Mexican war was overruled for good, inasmuch as it resulted in wresting, from a state of anarchy and misrule, a large portion of this continent, and bringing it under the empire of freedom. It does not require the spirit of vaticination to foresee, at this late hour of the day, that the whole of this New World, discovered by Columbus, is destined to be brought under that Empire of Freedom.

And who does not believe that this present great civil war, will be, in its results, as glorious for the family of man at large, as any that has ever preceded it, in the history of nations?

In the first place, it will be the overthrow of Slavery, which has so long been a withering and blighting curse to the richest and most beautiful section of our wide domain. If that should be

the only result, it will be worth all the blood
and treasure expended in the achievement of so
desirable an end.   In all my reading, I must
say, I have never read of a more matured system
of fraud, and wholesale murder and oppression,
than this system of slavery, which has been so
long tolerated under the auspices of our, so
called, free government.   For one, I rejoice for
my country, that it is to be blotted out forever.

In the second place, the effect of this war,
will be, to cement and strengthen the bonds of
the Union.   There is little probability that we
shall ever see another civil war in this land.   If
eleven powerful States, combining their resour-
ces and strength, could not succeed in breaking
up the Government, but have been so severely
punished for their mad undertaking, what likeli-
hood is there, that any other States will ever,
hereafter, venture upon a similar experiment?
No, we believe that all our sectional disputes and
differences that may hereafter arise, will be settled by ballots, and not by bullets.   There will
never be another appeal to arms to decide political questions and local disputes.   It is something, surely, to have attained a purpose so desirable as this.

In the last place, this war has served to developc the fact, that the people of this country have a government which can maintain itself, not only against foreign enemies, but against domestic focs, and traitors at home. The fact has been illustrated, that there is, in the heart of the masses of the people, a love for the Union, even stronger than love for life itself, which would cause them to rally to the defence of that Union, when endangered, under any and all circumstances. If this civil war were ended to-day, we should have no fears in regard to the perpetuity of the Union, not even if the Nations of Europe should conspire together, for its destruction. In view of the future of our country, which was also the country of Washington and of Franklin, we can say, *esto perpetua*, in the full belief, that the ejaculation is not uttered in vain.

We see, therefore, how it is, that the Almighty sends war, and overrules it, for the accomplishment of great good to the nations. Doubtless, all the wars that have ever occurred in the world, have resulted in some good, although shortsighted mortals might not be able to discover it, at the moment.

The Lord hath said, in his word, that, *he will*

overturn, and *overturn*, and *overturn*, till *he shall reign, whose right it is*, and *he will give him the kingdom.* The most obvious meaning of this language is, that revolution shall succeed revolution among the nations, until the reign of Jesus Christ is established, and then, there shall be peace on earth.

All the wars that have been waged of late years, and all the changes that are now taking place, in the condition of nations, seem ordained to prepare the way for the reign of Jesus Christ. The two last wars in Europe, the Crimean and the Italian, broke the power of the two most formidable despotisms in the old world. And this great American war, is destined to subvert and destroy Slavery, in the new world.

The reign of Jesus Christ, will be one of universal peace and freedom. Previous to the birth of Christianity, Slavery prevailed generally throughout the world. But it has been gradually retreating, as the Cross has advanced in triumph, till now. I believe there are but two countries under the influence of the Christian Religion, where slavery exists, viz; the Spanish West Indies, and Brazil, in South America. And it is known, that, it is but an imperfect form of Christianity that exists in those countries. But we may rest assured, that, it will not be many years before they will be fully redeemed from the curse, and the shackles shall fall from the limbs of every slave.

There are many signs which clearly indicate, that we are approaching the Millennial age of the world. Who can enumerate the discoveries and improvements in Science and Art, of the last fifty years, including the Steam Engine, the Rail Road, the Magnetic Telegraph, and a thousand other things, all of which are calculated to bring the scattered race of Adam nearer together, as one family, in the bonds of brotherhood and charity. And who can speak, in adequate terms, of the operations of the Press, in the diffusion of knowledge? The Bible has been translated into almost every spoken language, and millions of copies have been put into circulation.

Under this belief, of the near approach of the Millennium, I am willing to see revolution succeed revolution, in the affairs of nations. I rejoice to witness the great steppings of the Almighty on the theater of the world. Nor do I feel dismayed, at the fearful overturnings and

earthquakes, by which one gigantic system of
tyranny after another is overthrown. I believe
that we shall still hear of wars, and rumors of
wars, according to the word of Jesus Christ.
But, from the signs of the times, I believe these
wars will speedily take place, and it will not
be very long before the last battle shall be
fought.

England, Spain, and perhaps some other nations
have debts of long standing to be settled, which,
I think, will be exacted of them before very
long, in blood. If I know what justice is, and,
if I can read aright, there must be such debts
standing charged against them, in the Book of
the Most High, and when the hour for settlement comes, as come it will, they must meet the
account.

God does punish the nations for their sins!
Our nation, to day, in sackcloth and ashes, attests
the truth of this declaration. And if this favored
land has been so severely judged, will He, can
He, consistently with the principles of Eternal
Justice, let other nations escape? As sure as
God reigns on his throne in Heaven, he will not.
The innocent blood shed by them, will be ex-
acted of them, in turn.

There may be some now living, who, though not very young, may be permitted to see the last bloody conflict, which is to precede the dawning of the millennial day, when the olive branch of peace shall be seen throughout the world. The best commentators are of the opinion, that, the prophecies are nearly fulfilled, and that the commencement of that wished for, golden age of the world, is near at hand.

II.

WHAT IS SLAVERY?

To a conscience, humanized by the influences of a christian civilization, as well as to an enlightened reason, there is something repugnant in the theory, that one-half, or any portion, of the children of Adam, were born to be slaves and drudges for the other half. If the theory were true, one would suppose that men should come into the world, with some distinctive marks upon them, indicating to what destiny they were born.

We receive the Bible account of the creation of man; and, placing implicit confidence in the authenticity of that account, we cannot, for a moment, entertain the notion, that, during the first generation of man, even in the life-time of Adam, some of his sons and daughters were enslaved by the others, and bought and sold by them, as merchandise. But why not, if slavery is an Institution of Divine origin? Surely, we have a right

to suppose that every institution of a Divine nature—as marriage, and others which God established—must have flourished in the garden of
Eden, and during the earlier ages, when the world
was far more free from the effects of sin, than it
has been at any subsequent period; yet there is
nothing said of the existence of slavery in the
garden of Eden, and, in the Mosaic account of the
creation, there is no mention made of any such
institution.

We have learned men and eminent theologians
in our day, proclaiming the Divine origin of
slavery. They are, at this hour, edifying their
brethren throughout the Southern Confederacy, by
teaching that this new government has been ordained of God, for the purpose of conserving and
perpetuating the peculiar and Divine institution.
I am acquainted with one of these reverend lec-
turers. An Englishman by birth, he settled first
in Syracuse, N. Y., where he distinguished himself as an earnest and zealous advocate for abolition. Afterwards, he removed to the South, and
soon became equally earnest and zealous for the
divine right of slavery, and, months before the
war commenced, openly avowed and preached Secession from his pulpit.

Another lecturer, Dr. Palmer, is entitled to be considered as a leader in this class of divines. But he was born in South Carolina, and some allowance may be made for him, on account of the peculiar training and education he received in his youth. He asserted in a public discourse, .in New Orleans, that the cause of the Confederacy was a more just and sacred cause, than that for which Washington and the Revolutionary fathers fought. He also declared publicly, that, he should lose his confidence in God, as a God of truth and justice, if he should give success to the arms of the North. How strikingly we see verified, in such cases, the old heathen adage, " *Quem Deus vult perdere, prius dementat.*"

No, the most that can be said in favor of slavery is, that, like war and many other evils that afflict the world, it was engendered by sin. It belongs to the same family of ills that were let ·loose, when Pandora's box was opened, to scourge humanity. To say that it was ever designed as a blessing to the human family, would be, in effect to affirm that the curse which Noah pronounced on Canaan, *was a blessing!* It would be to put darkness for light; to call evil good. And to assert that slavery is a Christian Institution, would be tantamount to saying, that Christ did not come into the world to redeem men from under the *curse of sin*. But, to teach that the object of his Heavenly Mission to the earth, was to rivet the fetters of bondage on the slave, instead of breaking every yoke, is a piece of impiety bold enough to bring the blush of shame on the very cheeks of damnation.

No one, who makes any pretensions to piety, will controvert the position that slavery, as it exists, and as it has existed for long ages in the world, was originally produced by sin. It is one of the works of the Devil. But Christ came into the world to destroy the works of the Devil.

The principle that *might makes right*, is the principle that has practically governed the world, during Satan's dominion over it. It is the principle that has made slaves of one part of the family of man, and tyrants of another part of the same family.

The first slaves, as it is generally supposed, were captives taken in war, sold or distributed among the conquerors, and afterwards held by them as bondmen.

What would be thought by the civilized world, of any christian nation, who should sell the prisoners taken in war to be held as slaves for life, and their posterity? What would the philanthropists of England say, if our Government should cause the Confederate prisoners, taken in this war, to be sold into perpetual slavery? Yet, if slavery is a Divine Institution, and if it was just in its origin, we ought to do this; and certainly, no one could complain of the injustice, without finding fault with an ordinance of God! As a measure of retaliation, it might be viewed as an act of retributive justice, for their enslavement of the Africans. And we know that the law of retaliation is strictly just, although militating againt a dispensation of mercy, like that under which we have been brought by the Gospel. Dr. Palmer and his fellow laborers in preaching their new gospel, could not complain of our Government, if they should sell every rebel captured, himself included in the number, to be forever hereafter held as slaves.

But instead of fighting for such a principle, we make war against it, and it is nothing but opposition to this new and diabolical theory, that has involved us in this terrible civil strife, and clothed our nation in sackcloth.

What is slavery? Analyze the thing—Let its foul and corrupt carcass be dissected, and if any one can see in it, aught but sin, he must look through a medium strangely distorted.

What is slavery? Man puts a chain on the limbs of his brother man,—deprives him of his freedom—calls him his slave—and compels him, with whip in hand, to do his bidding! This is slavery!

Laws are enacted, legalizing the act, and giving him the right to hold his victim as a slave. Laws are enacted by the stronger party—the miserable slave has no voice in enacting the law; and is powerless to resist it—He is not now his own man—He belongs to another. He cannot use his feet any longer to walk whither soever he will. He is not at liberty to employ his hands to do whatsoever he will—He is not free to exercise his reason to choose and determine for himself, what actions are right—He has no right to the use of speech, to utter what words he may think most suitable—but every member, and every faculty of his mind and body, belongs to another; and he can only employ them, as instruments, to do the pleasure of another, whom he must call, *master*. This is *Slavery*. To say, that the Merciful Father willed it,—to call it a Divine Institution, may justly be considered as evidence of a perverted Intellect.

Has the wretched slave a wife now? Has he
a child? Has he a. father, or a mother? Has he
a legal right to cherish and protect his wife?
Can he live with, and support her, according to
God's Institution? Can he educate his child, and
train it in the way he should go, according to
God's Command? Can he comfort and support
his aged ·and infirm parents, as the dictates of
natural affection, and the duties of religion require?

No! he has no right to his own wife—no right
to his child—no right even to visit his old mother!
—His wife has been sold and is the slave, or the
mistress of another—His child belongs to another
master, and has been transported to a distant state,
and he shall never see that child again. This is
slavery! To call it a Divine Institution would
be to give utterance to that which would be nothing short of the boldest blasphemy.

Yet, this is the glorious Institution, for which
the Southern people made war against their brethren. For the inestimable privilege of holding a
portion of God's children in bondage, and carrying
on a traffic in the bodies and souls of men, they
rebelled against the ordinance of God, refusing to
" be subject to the powers that be."

They were prosperous and happy under the best Government the wisdom of man ever devised, but they were not content. They wished to carry chains and slavery into new Territory, and to propagate the curse, where it had never existed. And because they could not obtain a guaranty, from the Government, of immunity and protection, in the accomplishment of the damnable purpose, they stained their souls with the crime of Treason. This is one of the fruits of Slavery ! " Every tree shall be known by its fruit."

III

ORIGIN OF AFRICAN SLAVERY.

IF we may place any credence in the records of History, the first cargo of African Slaves was landed and sold in the island of Hispaniola, or St. Domingo. A severe retribution, as written in the subsequent history of that island, followed this invasion of the natural rights of man. Bancroft, in his inimitable work, remarks ; "Hayti, the first spot in America, that received African Slaves, was the first to set the example of African Liberty." For years, they have possessed and ruled the island, an enterprising and independent people. The tyrants, who held them in bondage, were put to death, or driven into exile, a significant display of the stern justice of Heaven!

The first slaves sold in the United States, then English Colonies, were brought from Africa, in a Dutch Man of War, which entered the mouth of James river, in the year 1620, four months before the landing of the Puritan pilgrims, on the rock of

Plymouth. So that, by a singular coincidence, the vessels of the same country, Holland, brought both the pilgrims and the slaves, to our shores, in the course of the same memorable year.

If we would fully comprehend the origin of slavery, in our land, it will be necessary to follow the kidnappers to Africa, and understand the manner by which they originally established their right of property in the bodies of African men and women. We must not forget that the claim of a *divine right* has been set up, in this age of progress. and reform.

If the kidnapper had a Divine warrant, or a special commission from Heaven, to alight on the shores of Africa, to murder and capture the defenceless inhabitants, and transport them to distant shores, as slaves, and if they could produce unquestionable evidence that they had such a commission, as the Jews could, when commanded by God to occupy the land of Canaan, we should be bound to pay some respect to the claim set up by the modern advocates of slavery. But I have never yet heard of any slave-pirate or kidnapper, who even pretended that he had such a warrant or commission from God Almighty, to steal the children of Africa, and sell them into bondage!

I have, however, heard of one Johnny Hawkins, a Sir knight, and a notable person in his day, who was the first Englishman who engaged in the traffic, and enlisted Queen Elizabeth to protect him in the same, and to share in the profits. But how did he obtain his right and title? He tells his own story. He does not intimate that he had any commission from Heaven. He went to an African village of eight thousand inhabitants. The huts were covered with dry palm leaves, very combustible. He set fire to these, which were, soon, all in a blaze. In the midst of the terror and confusion that ensued, he captured two hundred and fifty of the innocent natives, and had them conveyed, in chains, on board of his ship. This was his first cargo to Hispaniola, from which he realized a rich return, in sugar, ginger, and pearls. The profits were so immense, that, the government of the English nation resolved to engage in the trade. Bancroft says that the Sover-eign of England, "participated in the hazards, the profits, and the crimes, and became at once a smuggler and a slave merchant." The whole system had its foundation in crime and cupidity.

The slaveholders in our Southern States, obtained their right to own and hold these captured

Africans, as slaves, from Sir Johnny Hawkins, and others, who, like him, stole them from their native country. If the original kidnappers had no divine right to this species of property, it is a question, how those who purchased it from them, have come into the possession of such a right. If a thief has no valid right or title to the property, stolen by him, has the man who buys it of him, knowing it to be stolen property, a valid right or title to the same ?

I know that, as late as the year 1860, slaves were sold in Texas, Florida, and, perhaps, other Southern States, brought by kidnappers in pirate ships, direct from Africa, and, that some of these advocates for the Divine right of slavery, were the purchasers. I am not able to prefer any accusation against Dr. Palmer, as having been one of the number. But here is a question for him, and all of the same school of divinity, to consider : If the slaves owned by them at present, or at the time of Secession, were the children or the grand-children of those who were kidnapped in Africa, and to whom the kidnappers had no other claim than a thief's title, on what foundation do they now set up the claim of a Divine right? God shall judge these whited sepulchres ! They find their brother guilty of a skin not colored like their own, and they claim authority from King Jesus, to put a yoke of bondage on his neck, an iron chain on his ankle, and to make him their slave for life!

IV.

EARLY OPPOSITION TO SLAVERY.

WE must do justice to the Church of Rome, to say, that it has ever and persistently opposed the institution of slavery. Soon after the discovery of the New World, by Columbus, the Sovereign Pontiffs were repeatedly importuned to give their sanction, not only to the enslavement of Africans, but also, of the aboriginal inhabitants of America. But they never yielded to these importunities. Even as early as the twelfth century, when Mahometans enslaved Christians, and Christians, in turn, enslaved Mahometans, and slavery was all but universal, Pope Alexander III., in the genuine spirit of Christianity, wrote, in one of his bulls, *"Nature having made no Slaves, all men have an equal right to Liberty."* And after him, Pope Leo X. declared that, *"not the Christian religion only, but nature herself cries out against the state of Slavery."* Another Pontiff, Paul III., even went so far, as to imprecate the curse of God, on Europeans who should enslave Indians, or any other class of men. These are facts which ought to be borne in mind, especially by slave-holding Catholics in America.

The first ship which sailed from New England for the coast of Guinea, to trade for negroes, belonged to two men of Boston, whose names were Thomas Keyser, and James Smith ; but there was such a cry of indignation, raised against them, throughout the country, that they were arrested, and brought before a civil magistrate, as malefactors and murderers. The cargo of Africans, was ordered to be sent back to their native country, at the public expense, with a letter, expressing the indignation of the General Court, at their wrongs.

There was no slavery in Georgia, for years after it was first settled, and after it had been introduced into the neighboring state of South Carolina. . It was excluded, during the life-time of General Oglethorpe, the first governor, because of the earnest and determined opposition of that wise and good man. By the third regulation, adopted for the government of the colony, under his superintendence, slavery was absolutely pro-scribed. Oglethorpe himself wrote, "*Slavery is against the Gospel, as well as against the fundamental law of England. We refused to make a law, permitting such a horrid crime.*"

Many of the settlers earnestly requested, that the introduction of negroes might be allowed; and many even prepared to desert the colony, declaring that success was impossible without them. Notwithstanding, he sternly rejected their applications, saying, that he would have nothing further to do with the colony, if negroes should be introduced into Georgia. There is not a purer and more unblemished character, than that of Oglethorpe, among all those who had any thing to do with the settlement of the English colonies in America.

The name which stands highest on the roll of our Country's fame, is that of Washington. He has been claimed, as among the friends and patrons of the Institution of Slavery. It is true, it was his lot to have been born in a slave State, and to be involved in a connection with the Institution, by circumstances over which, perhaps, he had no control. His last will and Testament, shows how sincerely he desired the termination of slavery, in this country. In that will, this paragraph is contained,

"upon the decease of my wife, it is my will and
desire, that all the slaves whom I hold in my own
right, shall receive their freedom." The Will proceeds to specify, what provision should be made for
them, both before, and subsequent to the period of
their manumission; and he further enjoins on his
executors, to see to it, that this clause, respecting
his slaves, be religiously fulfilled at the epoch, at
which it was directed to take place, "without eva-
sion, neglect or delay."

If Washington was a defender of the Institution,
we have only to say it would have been a glorious
thing for our country, if all the planters in the
Southern States, had been such defenders and patrons of slavery, as he was, and had followed his
bright example. There would have been no division between the North and the South. There
would have been no civil war.

It is known that Thomas Jefferson was also a
slaveholder. But I am not aware that he has ever
been claimed as an advocate for the Institution.
He uttered prophetic words, when on one occasion,
speaking of slavery, he said, "I tremble for my
country, when I remember that God is just!" If it
was a prediction how fearfully it has been accomplished!

Jefferson penned the immortal document, which contains the declaration of our National Independence, and, we may suppose, that he expresses his own honest convictions, on the subject of slavery, in that complaint against the British Government, in which he says: "He [the King of England] has waged cruel war against human nature, violating its most sacred rights of life and liberty, in the persons of a distant people, who never offended him, captivating and carrying them into slavery in another hemisphere, or to incur a miserable death in their transportation thither. This piratical warfare, the opprobrium of infidel powers, is the warfare of the Christian King of Great Britain, to keep open a market where men should be bought and sold."

Jefferson did not profess to be a Christian; yet, if he had written under the influence of Inspiration, we know not whether he could have drawn a more vivid picture of the horrors of the slave trade. The same eminent statesman, also wrote to the planters of the south, saying, that they must emancipate their slaves, or "that something worse would follow."

It is known that he drew up the plan of a constitution for his native state, providing for the gradual extinction of slavery, but it was never adopted.

He was not a Christian, but he was a patriot, and
he has been called the "Father of the American
Democracy." He had studied deeply the principles
of human jurisprudence, and the essential laws of
right and wrong, and viewing slavery from that
stand-point alone, he saw and pronounced it a cruel
warfare against human nature itself, and a violation of its most sacred rights.

I will here, adduce the testimony of another eminent son of Virginia, against the institution of
slavery, viz., John Randolph, of Roanoke. It was
not the influence of Christianity, which made him
strike the fetters from the limbs of four hundred
bondmen, and put them in posession of the sweets
of liberty. But, he felt himself constrained to this
act of Justice, by that *innate sense of justice*, which, I
believe the Lord of the Universe, has implanted in
every heart. And though he performed this act of
justice, only when he was about to leave the world,
and had deferred, for a time, the doing of so just a
deed, yet the fact that he had deliberately made up
his mind to do it at all, and at last carried out the
intention, tells, more unequivocally than any words
he could have made use of, in what light he
viewed slavery. What is the reason the people
of Virginia have never paid any attention to the

lesson taught by his example? They feel a just pride in the memory of their Washingtons, their Jeffersons, their Clays, and their Randolphs; but ah! they heed not the voice of their words, nor the lesson of their example, no more than if they had been the most ordinary among men.

In vain, we search the records of the early history of our country, to find the name of one, among those who stood high as patriots, philanthropists, or statesmen, who was known, or was willing to be known, as the champion of slavery.

The first sentence in that incomparable document, the Declaration of American Independence, asserts this great and universal truth, "that God created all men free and equal, and endowed them with certain inalienable rights, among which are life, liberty, and the pursuit of happiness." This acknowledged truth, is the main pillar that supports, and will support the temple of our American freedom. It is because we did not understand this principle, as our forefathers understood it, that discord has reigned, of late, and that glorious temple has been shaken to its deep foundations, and well nigh overwhelmed in a mass of ruins.

We thank the authors and framers of that boasted Constitution, under which we have so long lived and flourished, as a nation, for not inserting the terms, *"slaves"* and *"Slavery,"* in that great *magna charta* of human liberty. In shaping and perfecting that noble instrument, why did they avoid the use of the term, *Slavery?* Evidently, because the thing itself signified by the term, was perceived, by them, to be utterly repugnant to the principles of a free government. Freedom and slavery are antagonistic ideas, and the logical mind, that has fully comprehended and embraced the one, must reject the other. They had a conscience, and that conscience revolted at the thought of taking the hideous form of slavery within their embrace, under the assumed name of freedom. They had a presentiment that the enlightened nations of the world would hiss at them, for affecting to lay the foundations of the most free and republican government on earth, and yet, denying to a portion of the inhabitants, every natural and political right of man. And, though they found the evil existing, and felt compelled to make concessions in favor of those who held men as property, they were not willing to let that great charter of a nation's rights be marred or deformed by the word slavery. And again, we thank them, for not permitting any such blot on that paper, which they drew up and signed, as the guarantee of all our rights and freedom, in all time to come. The American Constitution cannot be said to recognize slavery. The authors of it, cautiously and designedly kept the word out; and, as words are the signs of ideas, they kept out, and meant to keep out the thing signified by it.

Still, we are ready to admit, that, for the sake of harmony, the framers of that document, did enter into a kind of *tacit compromise*, in favor of the accursed institution. And, God in Heaven knows, that, if they were living now, they would shed bitter, scalding tears, at the recollection of the deed. The Almighty himself cancels the deed, and the disgrace of it is wiped out in a nation's blood!

V.

THE MIDDLE PASSAGE.

It has been estimated, that, during the three hundred years of the existence of slavery, more than forty millions of the children of Africa, have been brought, in slave-ships, to the shores of the new world, and sold into bondage. This does not include the number of those who were murdered in the capture, or died in the passage across the ocean. It has been said by those who had the means of knowing, that the latter number exceeds the former. But, supposing the numbers to be equal, Africa has lost eighty millions of her people, who have been made an offering on the altar of the slave-god. Of these eighty millions, ten millions, or one-eighth of the whole, are all that remain in existence. To this waste of human life, should be added the loss of the natural increase, under the rigors of bondage. It is known that the race is prolific, and under a mild system, founded on the natural principles of humanity, the forty millions transported to this country, ought to have doubled itself two or three times in the course of three centuries. If the laws of increase, from ordinary generation, had been in no wise hindered or checked, by the cruelty of the slave system, instead of ten millions, there must have been on this continent, at the present moment, in round numbers, a population of at least one hundred millions of Africans! It is fair, therefore, to put down the one hundred millions, as the sacrifice of human life that has been made to this infernal system! Think of this, O ye christians of the Free States! who are pleading with the Government, and pleading, in your hearts, with God Almighty, to spare the system, and who are bitterly denouncing the Government, because they have interfered with this social and domestic institution of their Southern brethren!

A few years ago, Lord Palmerston in the House of Lords, said :

"According to the report of Messrs. Vender-welt and Buxton, from 120,000 to 150,000 slaves are landed annually in America. It is calculated, that, of three negroes, seized in the interior of Africa, to be sent into slavery, but one reaches his destination, the two others die in the course of the operations of the slave-trade. Whatever may be the number transported, we must triple it to obtain the true number of human beings, whom this detestable traffic kidnaps every year from Africa.

"Indeed, the negroes destined for the slave-trade, are not taken from the neighborhood, where they are embarked. A great number come from the interior. Many are captives, made in wars excited by thirst for the gain procured by the sale of the prisoners. But the greatest number arise from kidnapping expeditions, and an organized system of man-stealing, in the interior of Africa. When the time approaches to set out with the slave caravans for the coast, the kidnappers surround a peaceful village at midnight, set it on fire, and seize on the inhabitants, killing all who resist. If the village attacked, is situated on a mountain, offering greater facilities for flight, and the inhabitants take refuge in the caverns, the kidnappers kindle large fires at the entrance, and those who are sheltered there, placed between death by suffocation and slavery, are forced to give themselves up. If the fugitive take refuge on the heights, the assailants render themselves

masters of all the springs and wells, and the un-
fortunates, devoured by thirst, return to truckle
their liberty for life. The prisoners made, they
proceed to the choice. The robust individuals of
both sexes, and the children from six to seven
years old, are set aside to form part of the caravan which is to be driven to the sea-shore. They
rid themselves of the children under six years
of age, by killing them on the spot, and aban-
don the aged and infirm, thus condemning them
to die of hunger. The caravan sets out, men,
women and children traverse the burning sands,
and rocky defiles of the mountains of Africa,
barefoot, and almost naked. The feeble are stim-
ulated by the whip, the strong are secured by
chaining them together, or by placing them under
a yoke. Many fall from exhaustion on the road,
and die, or become the prey of wild beasts. On
reaching the sea-shore, they are penned up and
crowded together in buildings, called barracoons,
where they fall a prey to epidemics. Death has
often cruelly thinned their ranks before the arrival of a slave-trader. The first who appears
takes his choice, setting aside the sick and feeble, and taking care always to take one-third or,
at least, one-fourth more than his vessel can hold,

and this, according to a mathematical calculation, for the same reason, that casks are put into a vessel loaded with wine, designed to compensate for the loss which will result from evaporation, or leakage ; for the captain knows perfectly well, that a large number of the negroes of his cargo will perish, some from grief, others from the change of diet, and many from Asphyxia.

"They do not, always, wait until the dying are dead, to cast them into the sea, but sometimes throw them overboard, as soon as they are hopeless."

Lord Palmerston then gives an incident of the kind which happened in 1738. "A man, named Collingwood was carrying slaves to Jamaica ; the ship took a wrong course, and water and provisions became scanty. Knowing, that, if the negroes died of famine, the owners would lose the insurance on them, while they would be entitled to this premium, if it were proved, that he had been compelled, by the perils of the sea, to sacrifice the cargo, the captain did not hesitate to precipitate one hundred and thirty-two living beings into the waves."

The distinguished orator then draws a description of a negro slave-ship, and quotes the words of a man who had seen one of these vessels, "a negro has not as much room in them as a corpse in a coffin."

From all these things, the noble lord draws the conclusion, that, if, one hundred and fifty thousand slaves land annually in America, the slave-trade carries away from Africa, three or four hundred thousands souls. According to him, "all the crimes of the human race, from the creation of the world, to our days, do not exceed those which have been caused by the slave-trade."

Bancroft, one of the most impartial historians, says, of the middle passage: "The horrors of the passage, corresponded with the infamy of the trade. Small vessels, of little more than two hundred tons burden, were prepared for the traffic, for these could most easily penetrate the bays and rivers of the coast, and quickly obtaining a lading, could soonest hurry away from the deadly air of Western Africa. In such a bark, five hundred negroes and more have been stowed, exciting wonder that men could have lived, within the tropics, cribbed in so few inches of room. The inequality of force between the crew and the cargo led. to the use of manacles; the hands of the stronger men, were made fast together, and the right leg of one was chained to the left of another. The avarice of the trader was a partial guarantee of the security of life, as far as it depended on him; but death hovered always over the slave ship. The negroes, as they came from the higher level to the sea-side, poorly fed on the sad pilgrimage, sleeping at night on the damp earth. without covering, and often reaching the coast at unfavorable seasons, imbibed the seeds of disease, which confinement on board ship quickened into feverish activity. There have been examples where one half of them, it has been said, even, where two-thirds of them, perished on the passage!"

The heart is made sick in reading such recitals! Can it be that those who claim to be called christians, approve and sanction such a trade? which Jefferson did not hesitate to stigmatize as "*an execrable commerce*," "*a piratical warfare*," "*the opprobrium of infidel powers*," and "*an assemblage of horrors*"! Yea, some of the most learned divines among our Southern brethren, (!) pretend to have a celestial warrant to hold their colored brethren in chains, to keep open a market for the sale and purchase of slaves, and to send the pirate ships annually on their dark way, to rob poor Africa, and obtain more victims!

I have never read a complete journal of any slave-ship, with her cargo, across the Atlantic. It has been said that no such journal has ever been published. If such a record had been kept and published, in all its details, it would, doubtless, have been a record of instructive interest, especially to the friends of the cause of slavery.

I can imagine that human genius would fail, in the attempt to give a just and vivid conception of the whole panorama on board of such a vessel, during the middle passage. It would take a pen, self-endowed with the mysterious and magical property of painting life-like pictures. Suppose they are heathens or savages, who are chained and crammed together in the hold of the ship, without sufficient light and air, naked and almost suffocated in the stench of human ordure and dead bodies; they are still human beings, endowed with the feelings of humanity. They had a country, and they have been torn away from that country. They had human affections, and they have been rudely separated from the embrace of all they loved. They are going to be slaves in a country they never saw—their hearts are broke!

Many die from grief, many from suffocation, many from disease caused by the noisome atmosphere. They are human beings, and, of necessity, many must perish. Could feeble humanity bear up under such accumulated sufferings, and yet survive? They die! the more sensitive and nervously constituted, fortunately for them! Happy they! whom the sea opens its friendly bosom to receive, and afford them repose from the tyranny and cruelty of man! Happy they! who die of a broken heart, murdered by men professing to be civilized! Millions are thus slumbering in their watery beds. The great and beneficent Father of all, has their broken hearts safe in His keeping. The sea will disclose its dead, and those innocent and outraged children of our common Father, will meet the slave-tyrants at the last, face to face! I believe it! I am thankful for this christian faith! If there is not a hell, there ought to be one!

VI.

THE LAST CRIME OF SLAVERY.

AT the lowest estimate which can be made, this civil war, by the time it shall be ended, will have cost the whole country, North and South, four thousand millions of money, one million of valuable lives, and a badge of mourning hung on nearly half the dwellings in the land. These are some of the fruits of the grand rebellion—and the cause of all is slavery!

There are copperhead patriots—thanks to him who first suggested a name so appropriate—who set themselves up as the apologists of slavery, and ascribe the war to the agitations of abolitionists, and other causes. I would make no appeal to their reason. I desire no discussion with them. There are none so blind as those who will not see. They are traitors at heart, less excusable than armed rebels at the South, and deserving of a severer punishment. They are not the friends of the Union. They appreciate not the blessings of a republican form of government. They cannot prize the advantages and the benign institutions of civil liberty, for the sake of what liberty is, intrinsically, in itself—and let them continue to bow down, and demean, as they have done, their pitiful souls, at the shrine of a low and contemptible personal ambition. The Vallandighams and Seymours of the North will get their reward, in the execrations of their children, in the next generation, if not sooner.

Look at that strutting congressman from South Carolina, the land of chivalry, par excellence. He thinks he can frighten and awe into submissive silence, by his blustering and bravado, half the numbers from the free States. He grew up from childhood with that disposition. The spirit began to run in his hot blood very early, and was quickened into a wonderful degree of celerity, by the training which he received.

That congressman was a slave-driver, with a whip in his hand, from the time he was four years of age. This is the way, and there is no mystery about it, that the children of all masters become bold and brave, and very chivalrous indeed. You will see young masters on nearly every plantation, who, from the time they begin to wear trowsers, strut about with whip in hand, a terror to all the young darkies on the lordly domain. If any should come in his way, crack goes the whip, and away go the young negroes, panic-stricken, and young master is already a young hero. This is the training they receive. And why should they not grow up to be knights of chivalry of the first order? A man is what he is made to be, whether he is made-right or wrong. We all know the truth of the poetic maxim,

" 'Tis education forms the common mind,
    Just as the twig is bent, the tree's inclined."

The young scions of chivalry are trained to be slave-drivers—and, tyrants by nature, this innate disposition is strengthened and developed by the whole course of training which they receive in early life—and how can they depart from it, when they are old? How can they be any thing else but tyrants, when they become grown men and women?

I have seen these young shoots of aristocracy in the common school, and I have seen them in colleges at the North and at the South, and every teacher has to deplore the fact, that, as a class, they lack the spirit of subordination, and, with rare exceptions, exhibit a domineering disposition, which may be said to be peculiar to the boys of the South.

There is hardly a faculty of any college in the free States, where there are ten or twenty young men from the South, who would not testify, if called on, that the management and control of these ten or twenty sons of chivalry, gives them more trouble than all the rest of the students in college. But still, they are the sons of wealthy planters, and usually bring a good deal of spending money, and they must bear some with their freaks and waywardness.

This is the beginning of that demoralizing influence, which slavery has on every mind, that comes in contact with it. The children are educated and trained up to be tyrants, and the effects are visible in every department and sphere of life, where they are called to act. In the national congress, their members bully and browbeat the members from the free States, and, as long as they can domineer over them, and control the action of congress, they are content to stay in the Union. But the very moment they are outvoted, and lose the ascendency in the halls of congress, they refuse to be any longer subject to the Government, and resolve to set up another Government, which they can manage or control for themselves. In short, wherever a body of slave-holders is to be found, they must be the ruling power. And it would be just as absurd to expect them to submit to the voice of the majority in a free Government, when that voice is pronounced by the people at large, as to expect them to relinquish their mastership over their own slaves, and submit to be governed by those slaves in turn.

But the demoralizing effect of slavery on the Southern mind, does not terminate here. The lordly master looks down, as it were, from an eminence, on the laboring classes as a servile and inferior population. Labor is, in itself, a badge of servility and inferiority. I do most positively affirm, after a residence of thirty years in the slave-States, that this is the light in which labor is regarded. The troops of General Butler had not been a week in New Orleans, before it was quite common for these young sprigs of aristocracy, male and female, to taunt the Yankee soldiers with their *plebeian origin.*

Negroes must work. They were made for that. They are fit for nothing else. They are an inferior race. This is the mode in which masters reason, and the inference is unavoidable—labor is a sign of degradation.

The son of a slave-holder does not labor, and he would think himself degraded indeed, if he were reduced to the necessity of having to work for his living.

The son of a planter might be an overseer, or a negro-driver, and he would not be degraded; but if he should learn a mechanical trade, and should work at that trade to earn a livelihood, he would be inevitably excluded from the upper class of society. They occupy a position so pre-eminently exalted above that of the slaves, that they cannot consent to be placed, in any sense, on a level with them. But to do, from necessity, the work of common laborers, is to put themselves in a condition so similar to that of the slaves, that they look on it as a state of degradation.

To give a clear and just conception of the prevailing sentiment, at the South, on this subject, I deem it expedient to quote a few sentences from several of their standard authors. Chancellor Harper says :

"In our own country, look at the lower valley of the Mississippi, which is capable of being made a far greater Egypt. In our own state, there are extensive tracts of the most fertilo soil, which are capable of being made to swarm with life. These are, at present, pestilential swamps, and valueless, because there is abundance of other soil in more favorable situations, which demand all, and more than all the labor which our country can supply. Are these regions of fertility to be abandoned at once, and forever, to the alligator and tortoise—with here and there perhaps, a miserable, shivering, crouching, free black savage? Does not the finger of Heaven itself point to a race of men, not to be enslaved by us, but already enslaved, and who will be in every way benefitted by the change of masters—to whom such climate is not uncongenial, who, though disposed to indolence, are yet patient, and capable of labor, on whose whole features, mind and character, nature has indelibly written—slave—and indicate that we should avail ourselves of these, in fulfilling the first great command to subdue and replenish the earth."

The last line in the above paragraph is an attempt to quote scripture, but it is both misquoted and misapplied. The sentence pronounced on man, was, "In the sweat of thy face, shalt thou eat bread till thou return unto the ground; for out of it wast thou taken; for dust thou art, and unto dust shalt thou return. Therefore the Lord God sent him forth from the garden of Eden, to till the ground from whence he was taken."

Now, whom did the Lord send forth, to till the ground? Was it the slave, or was it the slave's master? Inspiration teaches that it was *the man.* Who is meant by the man? The advocates of slavery are scarcely willing to admit that the slave is a man. We ought therefore to conclude that it was the slave's master who was doomed, when driven from paradise, to eat his bread in the sweat of his face.

Chancellor Harper would have expressed his meaning better, if he had said that the first great command was to subdue and enslave a portion of Adam's children, that we might avail ourselves of their labor, to subdue and replenish the swampy districts abandoned to the alligator and tortoise. Thus the slave would fulfil the curse, but the master would escape it. Was this the intention of Infinite Wisdom, when the sentence was uttered? If so, what fate, may we infer, was in reserve for the master? Let us hear what the same writer says on this point:

"The agriculturist or tiller of the soil, who can command no labor but that of his own hands, or that of his family, must remain comparatively poor and rude. He who acquires wealth by the labor of slaves, has the means of improvement for himself and his children. He may have a more extended intercourse, and, consequently, means of *information* and *refinement*, and may seek education for his children, where it may be found."

Now let us look at the plain, unvarnished meaning of this brief passage. The slave-holder is not to labor—not to till the ground with his own hands. He is to acquire his wealth by the labor of slaves—that he may have the means of *improvement* for himself and children—that he may have the means of *information* and *refinement*—and may be able to educate his children in the schools of Europe, or wherever education may be found. This was to be the employment

of the master and his children—not to toil—not
to earn his bread in the sweat of his face! But
here is a passage still more explicit, from tho
same distinguished writer.

"It is by the existence of slavery, exempting
so large a portion of our citizens from the necessity of bodily labor, that we have a greater
proportion than any other people, who have leisure
for intellectual pursuits, and the means of obtaining a liberal education." Aye, they were exempt-
ed from the necessity of bodily labor, but it was
done in contravention of the fiat of the Almighty.

Again, the same author observes—"It is better that a part should be fully and highly cultivated, and the rest *utterly ignorant.*" It is difficult to imagine that even one of South Carolina's
most gifted sons, should ever have penned such
a sentence. But here is still another choice paragraph from the same pen.

"We must avail ourselves of such labor as
we can command. The slave must labor, and is
inured to it; while the necessity of energy in
his government, of watchfulness, and of preparation and power to suppress insurrection, added
to the moral force derived from the habit of com-

mand, may help to prevent the degeneracy of the master."

What a lofty mission is assigned to the master! It is his to *watch* the slave—to be ever ready to suppress *insurrections*. And he must acquire the habit of *command*, and, therefore, he cannot degenerate for want of employment. What a noble mission is his! He can well afford to look down from his high position, on the common herd of drivelling laborers, and tillers of the ground.

Governor Hammond, of the same illustrious State, says; "It is impossible to suppose that slavery is contrary to the will of God." "I think, then, I may safely conclude, and I firmly believe that American slavery is not only not a sin, but especially commanded by God, through Moses, and approved by Christ, through His apostles." "I endorse, without reserve, that much-abused sentiment of Governor McDuffie, that slavery is the corner-stone of our republican edifice, while I repudiate, as ridiculously absurd, that much-lauded, but nowhere accredited, dogma of Mr. Jefferson, that "all men are born equal." And here is what the same distinguished orator says about the laboring classes in free countries :

"I affirm, that, in Great Britain, the poor and laboring classes of your race and color, not only your fellow beings, but your fellow citizens, are more miserable and degraded, morally and physically, than, our slaves; to be elevated to the actul condition of whom, would be, to these, your fellow citizens, a most glorious act of emancipation."

By this, he intended to say, that, if these laboring classes of Britain, could be sold to Southern slave-holders, and compelled to labor, under task-masters, like Southern slaves, their condition, moral and physical, would be so greatly improved, that it would be, as it were, a most glorious act of emancipation to them. He then asserts that the poor and laboring classes in the Northern Free States, are in a condition but a little more enviable than that of the laboring classes of England—that is, according to this authority, they are in a condition more miserable and degraded, physically and morally, than their African slaves.

We see, from these brief quotations, in what estimation, labor and an honest laboring population are held, and have been held, by these lordly and insolent nabobs of the South. Can it be said that slavery has not perverted their intellect, and

blinded their eyes? Was there ever a more striking verification of the old heathen philosopher's
saying, "Whom the Lord intends to destroy, he
first deprives of reason."

Once more, the baneful and corrupting influence
of slavery on the mind and soul of man, is seen
in the intense and almost fiendish hatred which
it engendered, in the Southern heart, against the
entire population of the North. I can say, that
hatred exceeded in virulence and malignity, any
thing I have ever known. The war was the unavoidable result. It was impossible that any people so thoroughly alienated from another, and ani-
mated by such a phrenzy of madness against them,
should continue to live under the same government
with them.

Two hundred men, according to the testimony
of the Hon. A. J. Hamilton, were hung in the
State of Texas alone, during the year 1860, for
no other crime than that of having been born at
the North. This was some months before the
State had seceded, and before it was known there
would be war.

The writer of these pages, would state, that,
during the same year, while traveling in the
same State about sixty miles from the place of

his residence, he was seized by a mob and would undoubtedly have been hung, had he not been able to procure certificates from some of the most influential men in the State, that he had resided thirty years in the South, and that he had never been known to be an abolitionist. I must here say, that, up to the moment of the bombardment of Fort Sumter, I had always been a conservative, and always conscientiously opposed to the agitation of slavery by the abolitionists. Gov. Hammond, in his work, "Slavery in the light of Political Science," said; "the only thing that can create a mob here, (as you might call it) is the appearance of an abolitionist, whom the people assemble to chastise; and this is no more of a mob, than a rally of shepherds to chase a wolf out of their pastures would be one."

Thus, we see that the people of the South had arrayed themselves against universal mankind. They bade defiance to the opinion of the civilized world. In their judgment, there was but one institution—slavery. That was the ultimatum of human hope and desire. And to that, every other institution and interest must succumb— Hear the same writer again: "you are stirring up mankind to overthrow our Heaven-ordained system of servitude, surrounded by innumerable checks, designed and planted deep in the human heart by God and nature, to substitute the absolute rule of this spirit reprobate, whose proper place was hell." " Come what may, we are firmly resolved that our system of domestic slavery shall stand."

The eloquent Dr. Palmer, of New Orleans, just before the State seceded, preached a discourse, afterward published in pamphlet form, in which he elaborated the proposition, that God had raised up the Southern people to conserve and perpetuate the institution of slavery; and on this ground he urged and advised secession.

O, there is no more melancholy spectacle, than to see a nation or an individual, thus poised on a giddy eminence, on their own narrow pedestal, and setting at defiance, the friendly warnings and the advice of the whole christian world! It is, and must ever be the sure precursor of a terrible and sudden overthrow. Where is Dr. Palmer now? Poising and trembling over the very abyss of atheism! He was known to declare publicly, before he fled from the presence of the Yankee troops in New Orleans, that, if the Almighty should favor the cause of the Yankees, he should lose his confidence in him as a God of truth and justice ! We cannot avoid the conclusion, that blindness of mind as well as a judicial hardness of heart, hath taken possession of the people of the South.

They were fully prepared to perpetrate the crime of treason. Slavery had schooled and prepared all their faculties of mind and soul for it, and all they awaited was a fitting occasion. This occurred on the announcement of the election of President Lincoln, the first President ever elected without the Southern vote. They even practised fraud and treachery to secure the election of Mr. Lincoln, that they might be furnished an opportunity for dissolving the Union. Their leading politicians knew, that, if Mr. Douglass were the nominee of the Charleston Convention, he would in all probability be elected, in which event, the Slave States, generally, would not follow South Carolina, in an attempt to dissolve the Union. Therefore, they determined to prevent the nomination of Douglass, so as to secure the election of Lincoln. I think that every intelligent man in the country, must know this state-

ment to be correct.   But I will here introduce
one fact in evidence.

In the State Convention of Alabama, which
met in Montgomery, to choose delegates to the
Charleston Convention, an exciting debate arose,
on the resolutions of instruction introduced, for
the guidance of those delegates, when they should
take their seats in that Convention.   By those
resolutions, they were required to vote for a
clause in the Democratic platform to be adopted,
permitting every slave-holder to carry his slave-
property to any part of the vacant territory of
the United States, where he might choose to settle.   Judge Hitchcock, of Mobile, one of the
members of the Convention, arose in his place,
and protested earnestly against the adoption of
such a resolution.   He told them, it was asking
too much of their Northern Democratic friends,
to require them to vote for carrying slavery into
all the vacant territory of the United States, and
more than the Northern Democracy were prepared to concede.   He warned them, that, to in-
sist on inserting such a clause in their platform,
would lead to a rupture in the Convention, and
probably to a dissolution of the Union.   And, in
closing his remarks, he told his friends, the mem-

bers of that Montgomery Convention, that they were on the verge of a precipice, and exhorted them to pause and consider, before they leaped, madly and blindly, into the abyss yawning before them.

They paid no attention to the words of warning which he uttered. William L. Yancey sprang to his feet, and exclaimed that he did not wish any gentleman to be deceived—that as for himself, he wanted it distinctly understood, that he was for a dissolution of the Union, "*with or without cause.*"

The resolutions of instruction were passed almost unanimously, there being but six votes against them, including that of Judge Hitchcock. The honorable gentleman was afterwards a refugee from his state for opinion's sake, and is now a presiding Judge in one of the Courts of New Orleans. Thus all things were made ready.

We come now to the final act in the drama. The lightning courier has carried the news throughout the length and breadth of the land, that Mr. Lincoln has been, duly and constitutionally, elected President for the next term of four years. What anathemas dire are poured forth from the press, and in every crowd and private circle throughout the Southern States! as if the cursing demon had been let loose from pandemonium! Liberal bets are offered that he would never be inaugurated. Threats are made that he never should be! The flag of the country is dishonored. It is hauled down from the towers and domes, in many a town and city, where it had ever proudly floated in the favoring breezes of heaven. That noble flag, the star spangled banner is trailed in the dust, by the maddened populace!

What terrible national calamity has wrought their passions to such a pitch of fury? What crime had Mr. Lincoln ever committed, or what Southern right had he ever assailed, or even threatened to assail? Not one. A man of unblemished reputation, he stands, and has ever stood by the constitution of his country, pledged by previous promises, and those promises renewed, and reaffirmed in the oath of office when he was inaugurated, sacredly to observe all the provisions of that constitution, and to guard and protect all the interests of the South, as all his predecessors had done. Why then did they secede? Why did they frantically disrupt the bonds of the best government ever enjoyed by man? Why did they venture to hurl themselves on the perils of a most bloody and fratricidal war? Can they assign any plausible reason? Let one of their own most distinguished statesmen answer.

"Pause, I entreat you, and consider for a moment, what reasons you can give to your fellow sufferers, in the calamity that it will bring upon us. What reasons can you give to the nations of the earth, to justify it? They will be the calm and deliberate judges in the case, and to what cause, or *one* overt act can you name or point, on which to rest the plea of justification? What right has the North assailed? What interest of the South has been invaded? What justice has been denied, and what claim founded in justice and right, has been withheld? Can either of you, to-day, name one governmental act of wrong, deliberately and purposely done by the Government of Washington, of which the South has a right to complain? I challenge the answer! Now, for you to attempt to overthrow such a government as this, under which we have lived for more than three-quarters of a century—in which we have gained our wealth, our standing as a nation, our domestic safety, while the elements of peril are around us, with peace and tranquillity, accompanied with unbounded prosperity, and rights unassailed—is

tho height of madness, folly, and wickedness, to
which I can neither lend my sanction nor my
vote."

The questions of Mr. Stephens have never been
answered — they cannot be! Nevertheless, the
work of demolition is begun. The temple of a
world's freedom, reared three-quarters of a century ago, must be destroyed. It is nothing that
George Washington laid the corner-stone in the
glorious structure, it must be razed to the dust!

They begin to muster the hosts of their chival-
ric Southern legions. The din and clangor of re-
sounding arms begins to be heard, and warlike
movements and preparations are seen on every
hand. They have counted the cost, and the die
is cast. They seize upon forts, arsenals, revenue
cutters, and other property belonging to the Government at Washington. They take possession of
custom houses, mints, and government funds, intended for the pay of the soldiers who had been
employed to defend their own frontiers, from the
depredations of hostile Indians. And the traitor,
Twiggs, even endeavored to force these faithful
soldiers into the service of the rebels.

Slowly, the government functionaries begin to
wake up, and to take measures to defend the

citadel of liberty. But they had slumbered a little too long. The torch of the incendiaries had already been applied. The flames were already kindled——and the mighty conflagration is not yet extinguished!

When we review the whole matter, we are overwhelmed with amazement, and penetrated with the deepest sorrow, to know that there should be found concentrated so many of the elements of depravity, and in such strength, in the hearts of a whole people. They will never be able, hereafter, to assign to their consciences, or to their children, a single satisfactory reason, for this mad rebellion, against the legitimate and ordained governments of Heaven and earth. They cannot plead, that it was because their institutions were insecure, or were threatened. The earnest and eloquent voice of their own Stephens, would be a refutation of any such plea.

Long ago, the great statesmen, John Q. Adams, conjured them to adhere to the Union, as the only means of maintaining their cherished institution of slavery. The compromise ingrafted on the constitution, unfortunately for the whole country, was their guarantee of safety, as to that institution. The national congress never would, never could have interfered with slavery in the States where it exists, so long as that constitution remains unchanged. And there was not the slightest probability of any such change being made, at least for half a century to come.

The rebels knew, moreover, that even should they succeed, as they had little reason to expect, in effecting a permanent dissolution of the Union, and establishing their separate independence, their slave property could not be half so secure, as under the old Union—that all fugitive slave laws would be repealed, and that there would be a *Canada frontier* erected on every side of them.

What, then, did they hope for—what could they have hoped for, from a change? They were spellbound! They were under the influence of an awful delusion! We must believe that the vengeance of a justly offended Deity was suspended over them, which made it necessary that the accumulated crimes of slavery, should be expiated in their blood! The time, decreed in the secret purpose of God, had come, and the bitter cup which they had prepared for their own lips, they must drink; aye, to the lowest dregs!

VII.

THE EXPIATION.

THERE is an established connection between sin and suffering. I believe it is a necessary and universal law, ordained by God Himself. This nation has been severely judged. The judgment has been brought on us directly by slavery, and, therefore, they stand related, the one to the other, as *cause and effect*. By this rule, we may determine in what light the system of slavery is regarded by the Supreme Being. Let us contemplate and fairly comprehend this important and fixed law of His Providence.

We believe that nations, as well as individuals, are punished for their crimes. And we believe, further, that they are not punished, except for crimes committed against His law. And if we believe this, we cannot be in doubt, as to what is the Divine verdict in reference to slavery.

All men, and all nations, which are not atheists,

act with implicit confidence in the truth of the belief, just stated. It has been the practice of nations, from time immemorial, in seasons of general calamity, and under the reverses of war, to humble themselves for supposed national sins, and to appeal to their deities, to avert from them the calamities, actual or threatened. Would this be the case, universally, amongst heathen as well as Christian nations, if there were not, in the minds of all, a general belief that there is a connection between the judgments with which nations are visited, and the sins for which they are thus visited, in the Divine displeasure? Ye, who profess to be civilized and Christian freemen, how long will ye ignore this universal belief, and this knowledge of the laws of the Divine Providence, according to which he deals with nations, and blesses them, or curses them, in the just ratio of their deserts!

We know that the system of domestic slavery in the South, brought this war upon the country. Have we yet learned to regard the war in the light of a national punishment, inflicted on the nation for the crime of slavery? Has there ever been a day appointed for national humiliation, fasting and prayer, on account of this sin? Never!

Has an order ever gone forth to the army to abolish slavery in the conquered districts, on the ground of the moral turpitude and sin of the system? Never! Has the nation, as such, ever repented, or even professed the necessity of repentance for this gigantic national crime? Never!

Many of the politicians at the North, even some of their hypocritical preachers, and a large portion of the citizens in all the States, are still disposed to be the apologists of this masterpiece of hell's workmanship, and would gladly take back their Southern brethren into their loving embrace, with this darling sin still clinging to them, if the Lord would permit them.

The judgments may be expected to continue till the nation is humbled, and repents of that great crime for which it is punished. They, therefore, who put themselves forward as apologists for the sin, are the real enemies of the country, and are standing in the way, between us and pardon, and reconciliation with the offended Deity. We shall never have peace, till slavery is abolished. The Lord is chastising us as a people for this sin, and we cannot repent of the evil, without putting it away.

We shall see, that, if anything is accomplished

by this war, it will be the destruction of slavery.
The nation will be corrected—the country will be
purged—and we do not expect to see the termination of this war, till that great end, for which
the war was sent, is accomplished. If we had
understood this at the beginning, the war could
have been terminated in six months. If the proclamation of emancipation had gone forth at the
very commencement, and if the commanding gene-
rals of the army had been permitted to muster
the enslaved into the army, to assist in the cause
of emancipation, the South could never have organized a powerful army at all. The sons of
chivalry would have been kept at home, to defend
their own hearth-stones from domestic insurrection. The Southern people have always stood in
dread of their slaves. It was their weak point.
But the North seemed entirely to ignore the fact,
and the Government refused to aim a decisive
blow against that weak-point. They resolved, at
first, to crush the rebellion, and yet spare the peculiar institution. They tried the experiment, but
made a failure. They had yet to learn that they
had grappled with a monster.

The first call was for seventy-five thousand
men. The second call was for an army of half

a million. They saw the flower of this army swept away. A thousand millions of treasure had been expended, and the Government saw they were no nearer the accomplishment of their object than when they began. At last, from very necessity, they adopted the policy of emancipation, compelled thereto by an overruling Providence!

Now, who has stood in the way of victory? Is it the Government, or is it the people?

Suppose the proclamation of freedom had come out at the very beginning of the war, what a storm of indignation would have been raised by the Northern people against the President! They did not desire the overthrow of slavery.—They were not prepared for the measure—and the Government dared not to move too fast. But I ween that by the time the nation has bled enough, they will have become quite orthodox on the question of slavery.

I think I have shown, with sufficient clearness, that this war was caused by slavery—that it is the fruit of slavery. We ought to be able to judge of a tree by its fruit. But more on this point anon.

History teaches us that nations are punished for their sins. A profound Christian faith convinces us, that no nation can violate the laws of Heaven and of eternal justice, with impunity. I need not cite examples from history, for I should have to instance all the nations, whose history is known, which have been scourged; which have been desolated by fire and sword; which have been brought to the verge of extermination, time and again; and show that in every case, it was because of their national wickedness in the sight of Heaven, and their disregard of the rights of justice and humanity.

The connection between national crime and national calamity, is better traced in the history of the Jewish nation, than any other, because the pen of Inspiration has pointed out the connection. But we may not suppose that other nations, offending against the laws of the universe, have been dealt with, by a different rule. If some inspired pen had been provided to write the tragical history of the nations that have passed away, or that are existing still, in a languishing and broken condition, pointing out, in every case, the causes of the desolation of one; the convulsion of another; the severing into fragments of a third; the utter blotting out of a fourth, etc., as the inspired writers have done in the case of the Jewish nation, we should be in possession, for our guidance, of an ever present mentor, to whose voice, if we were indifferent and inattentive, we should deserve to forfeit our national prestige and glory, and even to have our name blotted out.

But, as a nation, professing to be Christian, it is enough for us to know that war is the red hand of the Almighty, with which he punishes and scourges the nations for their iniquities. And we ought to know that we are now suffering the vengeance of Heaven, on account of slavery. This can be made evident by several considerations:

1. Slavery was the cause of the war. This was the point insisted on in the preceding chapter. It is no longer a debateable question. We suppose that there is no well informed person in the land, who would deny the fact. Slavery was the original and primary cause of the war. If then there had been no slavery, there had been no war. For the cause ceasing to exist, the effect ceases, of course.

But slavery exists, and it has produced the war. It is the most fearful calamity that has ever fallen on the nation. It has clothed the land in mourning. It flouts on its blood stained banners, unmistakable signs of God's anger against us as a people. The crimson tide of life, from sons and brothers, has moistened many fertile plains and valleys. We are threatened with the loss of our nationality, and our national glory—all, all because of slavery! Can it be that so much of evil and suffering to a whole people, should have its origin directly and solely in a cause, in itself, just, holy and good? Would this be in accordance with the principles of the Divine Government? To maintain the affirmative would be impious. The character of the effect, shows the character of the cause. And by this rule, slavery is condemned. By the same rule, we learn what is the 'verdict of the great monarch of the universe 'concerning it.

2. The final and only important result of this war, will be the destruction of slavery. If the nation is successful in the struggle to maintain its very existence, this end will be inevitably attained, although not originally intended or designed, by either of the contending parties. The cherished institution of the South will be blotted out. Can we think of any other important and radical change, that will be made in our constitution and

our government, but this? All our other civil and religious institutions, founded in wisdom and piety, will remain to us unimpaired. Commerce and trade, and all the arts of a great and Christian people, will receive a new impetus, and flourish as formerly. Our free schools, a free church, and a free press will be continued, still to bless and enlighten the millions of freemen, who shall be raised up to inhabit this goodly land. The nation, by its recuperative, self-inherent energies, will soon recover from the effects of the mighty shock, and settle down again on its former basis of unexampled prosperity. There will be no visible change. But slavery will have passed away. And there may be an alteration in the constitution adapted to this new state of things. Can we discern nothing in this, indicative of the will and intentions of that overruling Providence that controls all events? Or can we suppose that the God of this nation will not do all his pleasure?

3. The evils of this war, viewed in the light of a national punishment, fall heaviest on those guilty of the sin of slavery. This is another manifest indication, as to what is the Divine intention concerning it. Where punishment is inflicted, justice requires that it fall on the guilty.

In the first place, the theatre of war has been mainly in the Slave States. It is their fields which have been desolated, and drenched in blood. It is there, where the poor slave has so long clanked his chains, that the once rich and cultivated tracts have been devastated; that towns and villages have been sacked and burned; that thousands of once happy homes have been forsaken, and tens of thousands of delicate wives and daughters of planters, have been reduced to a state of starvation, and of the utmost destitution, by the accidents of war.

Again, we may safely estimate, that the sacrifice of human life, will amount, by the time the war is closed, in round numbers, to one million of men, divided about equally, between the North and the South, who have fallen in the field, or by diseases caused by exposure and privation in the service. It is known that many entire regiments, in the rebel army, were reduced to one-half their original number, before the end of the first winter campaign. This is a fearful waste of human life. The loss of half a million, out of a population of seven million white inhabitants, would be fully one-half of their able-bodied fighting men; whereas, the same number deducted from the twen-

ty-one millions of the Northern States, would be
equal to but one in six, who have fallen victims
to the war. How unequally has the punishment
fallen! The Slave States have lost half their men,
who were able to bear arms; the Free States
have lost one-sixth part. There is a Providence
in it, to whose voice we may not turn a deaf ear,
if we would.

In the third place, the fortunes of the Southern
people have been swept away, as chaff blown by
the wind; while the people of the Free States,
with few exceptions, have been as prosperous
and thriving, as at any former period in the history of the country. It is melancholy to contemplate the change which a few brief months
have wrought in the condition of the whole South,
and its inhabitants.

Many, who, a short time ago, were millionaires,
will be made beggars. The exactions of Jeff.
Davis, to carry on the war, and maintain his authority, have already stripped the most of them
bare. Their wives and daughters, who had been
accustomed to ride in elegant carriages, and flaunt
their silks and jewelry, are reduced to rags. In
many cases, their children, the offspring of aristocracy, cry for bread, to appease their hunger. It

is known that the armies at Vicksburg, and at Port Hudson, for some days before they surrendered, had no meat but mules' flesh; and that the latter army, under General Gardiner, did not surrender till they had eat the last mule.

Now, if we suppose that there is a Providence in all this, how terrible is the doom that has fallen on the heads of the slave-holders! At the close of the war, they will find that their slave property, on account of which they made the war, is gone. The little remnant of their property, which Jeff. Davis had not extorted from them, will be confiscated on account of their treason. Their families, who had never labored, and had been brought up to despise labor, will be in a condition utterly destitute and helpless. I can think of no other instance of the Divine displeasure, which affords any analogy to this, but that of the ancient Egyptians, whose first-born were slain by the destroying angel; whose cattle were destroyed by the plagues; whose army was overwhelmed in the Red Sea, on account of the sin of oppression.

In the last place, perhaps, the bitterest ingredient in the cup of retribution, hereafter, will be the reflection, "we brought the ruin on ourselves!"

I believe that the madness of the hour will pass away. I believe that reason will again ex- ercise her wonted sway, when there will come a bitter, but unavailing repentance. Then they will recall to their recollections, the advice and faith- ful warnings of their Alexander H. Stephens, their Crittenden, their A. J. Hamilton, and even their Sam Houston, and a few other wise states- men, who truly and clearly pointed out, what would be the consequences of their rebellion. They will be compelled to remember how pros- perous and happy they had always, been, under the old government—that no rights of theirs had ever been invaded by that government—that the old constitution had always protected them in the possession of their slave-property, and would still have afforded them protection, if they had not madly and wickedly chosen to put themselves forever beyond that protection. If any of them go into exile in other lands hereafter, these will be their reflections—that they had a country whose flag was honored in every land; that they had wealth and friends; that they were prosper- ous and happy; that they had not known what oppression was. And will not such thoughts as these, be intensified even to agony, when they

shall see that well known flag at the mast head
of American vessels, in the ports of the different
countries, where they may be exiles, still·honored
and respected, by all men, as the symbol of freedom? How fearful, but just are the retributions
of thy Providence, to the wicked, O God!

But why should the innocent suffer with the
guilty? For it cannot be denied that the inhabitants of the States in which slavery did not exist,
have already suffered, and must still suffer from
this war. Why are they made to share in the
punishment due to the sins of others? The answer is, the nation is responsible for the existence of the system of slavery, and the expiation
of the guilt thereof, is justly required from the
whole nation.

It is true, the body of the people in the Northern States, years ago, saw and deplored the evils
of the system, and emancipated all their own
slaves. So far, they did well. But still, the
institution of slavery at the South, with all its
peculiarities and enormities, has grown up and
flourished under the auspices and shadow of the
great American tree of liberty. A recognition of
the system was engrafted upon the Constitution,
and it has been recognized and protected by the

American Congress. Therefore, it may be said that the Sovereign Ruler of nations, justly holds our Government responsible for the existence of the evil. Who, then, shall complain, that the nation feels the rod of chastisement, lifted for the correction of the whole people.

Not only was the Government a guilty party, in entering into a compromise or treaty, recognizing the system, and incorporating it into the body politic, but the entire people of the North, have liberally patronized and encouraged the institution, in purchasing cotton and sugar, the products of slave-labor. These articles, it may be affirmed, were the sweat and blood of African slaves, extracted from them by the lash of task-masters, who were utterly destitute of the feeling of humanity! And yet the Christian people of the North, and the people of England, protesting all the while against the barbarities of the system, would purchase these articles.

Let England continue, hypocritically, to protest against slavery, the world knows that her immense commerce and trade, is, in great part, maintained by the toil of slaves. She is the most liberal patron of the system, and, if she dared, she would, to day, recognize the Southern Confederacy,

and aid in laying the foundations of a slave-re-
public, for the sake of a monopoly of the trade
of that republic. O England, tremble in view of
the fate that surely awaits thee! God is just, and
there are many sins laid to thy charge, yet una-
toned for!

I have endeavored to ascertain the purpose of
the Divine will, so far as that purpose can be
known by the dispensations of his Providence in
the present war; and, according to my honest
convictions, there seems to be but one conclusion
to which every good man and christian must come,
viz: that it was intended as *a righteous and just
judgment for the sin of slavery.*

If I am wrong in this conclusion, I would despair of ever being able to read aright any lesson,
taught by the dispensations of the Divine Providence, in the management of human affairs.

If I am right in the conclusion to which I have
arrived, what is our duty, as a people? Mani-
festly, it is to confess and repent of *this sin*, as a
nation! We have not yet done this. It is true,
that days for fasting and humiliation have been
appointed. But this has been, *pro forma*, and
from custom, rather than from any deep conviction
of the great guilt of that peculiar system of ini-

quity, on account of which the nation is scourged. Can that repentance be acceptable in the sight of heaven, in which there is not even an acknowledgement of sin?

It is true, that individual christians have long deplored the existence of the evil, and made confessions on behalf of the Government. But when has the Government itself ever taken this position? Never! If our rulers will not get down in dust and ashes to humble themselves before the Almighty for this sin, let the people set them the example. Let petitions, signed by thousands, be at once addressed to the President, praying him to appoint a day, to be observed as a day of humiliation and prayer by the nation at large, calling on them especially to make confession and repent of that particular form of sin, for which the nation is judged, viz: *the sin of slavery*, if by any means, they may be able to avert the just anger of heaven.

If a proclamation like this were to emanate from the White House at Washington, it would be as welcome to millions of pious hearts, as the rising of the star of hope, or as the dawning of the day of salvation to our distressed and bleeding country! We should begin to think that the

Lord's anger was already appeased, and that He was just about to return to its sheath again, the sword drunk with the blood of nearly a million of lives!

VIII

THE "MALUM IN SE" THEORY.

A STATE of ignorance may be said to be the normal condition of the human mind. And yet all the guides and teachers which the Author of our being has ordained for the instruction of man, teach the way of truth without error. All the voices of nature, not less than the voice of Revelation, incessantly proclaim to him, where the temple of truth is situated, and may be regarded as so many indices, pointing him in the road that leads thither.

Truth rests upon a firm and immovable basis. There is not a truth, that is not as clear as the sunlight. There is not an error in the world, that has any firm support for its foundation. But every error is an illusion, the result of false appearances, and maintained by false arguments and testimony.

Why, then, does man—why do all men so eagerly embrace error, rather than truth? Alas! the intellect is clouded by sin, and to that extent, the natural understanding has been brought in subjection to the power of sin. The philosophy of the whole subject, is best explained in those inspired words, "Men love darkness rather than light,"—that is, error rather than truth—"because their deeds are evil." If the hearts of men were not evil, they would not hate truth—they would not be averse to the light, and they could not love darkness more than the light. But their hearts are evil, and to evil inclined—and this affords the only true solution in the case.

Look at the thousands of creeds, and systems, and theories that have, at one time or another, prevailed in the world. One system, one theory, one creed after another passes away, only to give place to other systems, and creeds, and theories, which, in like manner, soon explode, and prove to be no more real or substantial than a bubble, on the surface of the waves.

Where is the system of religion in the world, that does not contain in it, a hundred errors to one truth, except the system taught in the Book of books? Where is the system of human philosophy, that has stood the test of time, or that

was not erected on a foundation of falsehood?
Where is the theory of human government, that
has not proved defective, and soon been changed
for some other theory? Where is the book, written by uninspired man, worthy of attention at all,
that has not inculcated a vast deal, nay, a thousand times more of error than of truth? Do we
not know that the philosophies of men are as
ephemeral and short-lived as their authors? The
philosophies of one age, give place to those of
the succeeding, which are substituted in their room,
and these again are overturned by still newer systems, which spring up in the next age. And so
the world wags on.

How crooked and diverse are the paths of error!
Men are continually changing! The man of to-
day, can hardly be said to be the man of yester-
day! But TRUTH NEVER CHANGES! Truth is eternal! This sentiment cannot be too deeply inscribed on our heart and memory.

How comes it, that, while one, self-erected into
a philosopher or teacher of mankind, pronounces
all slavery a sin—a *sin per se*—and the very relationship between master and servant to be sinful;
another, equally as wise in his own conceit, and
confident in his ability to instruct and enlighten

his fellow-men, pronounces the institution of slavery to be one of Divine appointment, designed for the highest good of our race, and intended to be perpetuated to the end of time? Can both theories be true? Can either of them be true? No fact can be better established than that both are alike founded in error. And yet, it was *the conflict between these two opposing theories*, that has involved our unhappy country in this dreadful civil war.

I cannot now say that I blame the abolitionist, for the instrumentality he has had, in alienating the people of the South, and plunging the country into a war. For, I think, I see now, that he was but an instrument in the hand of the higher Power.

The war might have been averted—perhaps, I may say the war would never occurred, but for the conflict between these opposing theories, of which I have spoken. In fact, all wars result from the conflict of opinions amongst men. It is the way in which such disputes, when they assume a national character, are usually settled.

Perhaps, the war might have been averted. But then, how would the Most High have executed his decree of vengeance? For, that He had formed such a decree, to punish this nation for all the crimes and bloodshed of which they had been guilty in perpetrating the horrors of the African slave trade, and in patronizing and upholding the accursed system, for so many years, I believe as firmly as that He occupies the throne of universal dominion. Still, while I make this declaration, I at the same time freely admit, I feel no regret, that it was the abolitionist and not myself, who was employed as the instrument in bringing to pass the accomplishment of that decree of wrath, at the fulfilment of which the nations of the earth stand aghast.

If the abolitionist had been content simply to denounce the African slave-trade—If he had only warred against the system of slavery existing in the Southern States, as, *in many of its features*, and *under the existing laws and regulations of those States subversive of the rights of humanity, and contrary to the principles of the Divine will, as made known in his word*, I for one should never have had any cause of disagreement with him, provided he had conducted the controversy in a christian spirit.

But when he went beyond. this, and began to teach a new philosophy, advocating the *malum in se*, theory, in reference to slavery, he assumed a position from which he was compelled to draw a

line, even through the church of the Lord Jesus
Christ, excommunicating in a body, all slave-
holding christians, with whom fraternal and christian communion had been maintained, ever since
there has been a church on earth. He introduced
a new test of christian character, which neither
Christ nor his apostles had ever instituted, as a
necessary qualification for the communion of the
church ; and had he lived in the days of the apostles, he would have excluded many from the
church, whom they retained in it. For it is not
denied, that, among the various communities, to
whom Paul, and the other apostles addressed
their epistles, there were slave-holding christians.
But no where, in any of their epistles, do we find
any intimation, that they were to renounce all
connection with slavery, or, in other words, to
liberate their servants or bondmen, as a necessary qualification for the communion of the church.
There is not a sentence in any of those epistles,
from which the inference can be logically drawn,
that all slavery is a sin, which must, therefore, be
classed with murder, theft, adultery, drunkenness,
and other such like abominations, which are sins
at all times, no matter under what circumstances
committed.

Further, this new and extraordinary dogma, would have excluded from the favor of God, and from the hope of salvation, the ancient patriarchs, and founders of the Jewish Church, Abraham, Isaac, and Jacob, who, we know from the Divine Record, were the proprietors of immense numbers of servants, both of those whom they had raised, and whom they had bought with their money. Nay, the same theory necessarily arraigns the wisdom of the Divine Legislation, in establishing slavery, by express command, among the Hebrews, in the land of Canaan, after the original inhabitants had been dispossessed and subdued. For these and other reasons, I never did, and I do not now, adopt or endorse that theory.

Let us look, for a moment, at the effects of the promulgation of that dogma. It cannot be denied that ecclesiastical bodies have been rent asunder and divided, Northern christians refusing all fellowship and communion with Southern christians, because of the sin of slavery. And if *the unity of the body of Christ was destroyed, under the effects of this preaching,* was it reasonable to expect, or to hope, that the body politic could remain one and indivisible?

As soon as the abolitionist had adopted the

malum in se theory, and had made himself sure of the truth of it, that moment, he lost all fraternal and charitable sentiments towards Southern christians, or those involved in a connection with slavery. He began to regard them as heathen and as sinners. The very fact of their owning a slave, was sufficient proof to him, that they were still in an unchristian state—still "in *the gall of bitterness, and the bond of iniquity.*" Of course, he felt himself justifiable in denouncing them as "*kidnappers,*" "*man-stealers,*" "*robbers,*" as men "in covenant with hell and in league with death," etc., etc. Prior to the date of the promulgation of that dogma, Christian charity forbade that any class of communicants should be thus denounced. But as soon as the abolitionist had got in possession of a principle, which excluded this class all from the church, he might, without any great inconsistency, begin to employ harsh and bitter words, and to *treat as heathens,* those made such by his own philosophy.

The legitimate fruit of these bitter denunciations, and this altered style of address, towards the South, was soon apparent. As might have been anticipated, it caused irritation. A feeling of alienation between the two sections of North

and South was engendered. That alienation has
increased and strengthened, from the first moment, up to the present time. Hatred against
the abolitionists has become the passion of the
Southern people—an intense hatred, which I can
only describe as fiendish!

Of course, no one would undertake to justify
the people of the South for thus having the worst
passions of their nature aroused, and giving themselves up, on so slight a provocation, to the absolute possession of such vindictive passions. I
am speaking of the results that followed from the
propagation of the"*malum in se*"theory. Neither
would I assert, that, it was the *aim* of the abolitionist, to produce these results. It might have
been—it probably was, his design, simply, by ad-
monition, by warning, by rebuke, to point out to
slave-holders, the enormity of their guilt, and
lead them to put away the sin of slavery.

If this was all the abolitionist designed, the
design was honorable and upright. But it is
quite certain that he erred, in the use of the language and manner employed, for the accomplishment of his design. Human nature is the same
the world over. Men may be persuaded—they
can even endure the language of remonstrance

and rebuke, when spoken in kindness. But they cannot be driven to any measures of reform, no matter how necessary. And they rebel and turn upon their assailants, when attacked by opprobrious and insulting epithets.

Another effect, which followed the violent course of the abolitionists, was to put slave-holders in an attitude of self-defense, in regard to their peculiar institution. They began to use weapons and arguments which they had not previously employed. Not only did they close their eyes and their ears to all appeals and all arguments coming from a Northern source, but they set themselves diligently to study the arguments on their own side of the question, and soon began to acquire a wonderful facility in converting even the shallowest sophisms into the most convincing arguments, for the Divine origin of slavery.

Parson Smiley, of Mississippi, was the first, I believe, who attempted to defend the institution, upon Bible authority. He brought out his pamphlet in the year 1837. I was residing in Natchez, at the time, and I remember well, what were my own sensations, and how other ministers among his brethren, seemed to be grieved by the boldness of this attempt to sustain such an institution, by an appeal to the word of God. The impression seemed to be, that, it would seriously and injuriously affect the whole Church, especially in the South. But the pamphlet had its influence. People read it—the quotations, arguments, and inferences, all seemed to be plausible and apposite. And soon there were not a few among the more intelligent and wealthy of the population, who were willing to accord to Mr. Smiley, the honor of having written an unanswerable defense of their cherished institution. From time to time, since, other productions of a similar nature have been published, till now, there is scarcely any gentleman's library in the South, that is not well-stocked with volumes, advocating the Divine origin of slavery. Not one slave-holder, perhaps, in a hundred, could be found who would presume to question the Divine right, or the morality of the institution. Such, and so great is the change, that has taken place in the public sentiment at the South, on this exciting topic, within a period of less than thirty years.

I cannot say that I am prepared to affirm, that this sudden and rapid change, on a subject of such absorbing interest, was wholly a reactionary result, produced by the measures adopted by the extreme abolition party in the North. I only state, what appear to me to have been, the facts in the case. One thing, however, I will affirm; and it is, that, up to the date above mentioned, there were few pious men in the Church at the South, or even among the more intelligent planters, who did not freely admit that slavery is an evil. They usually qualified the admission, however, by saying that it is a *necessary* evil, and unavoidable in certain conditions of society.

Thus, the conflict between opinions, North and South, was initiated. Churches have been divided by lines running parallel with Mason's and Dixon's line. A spirit of irreconcilable enmity has been engendered, between the people of the two sections. And now, we behold this once and long favored land, desolated with fire and sword, and drenched in fraternal blood. *"Behold how great a matter, a little fire kindleth!"*

Can we suppose that such direful calamities to Church and State, could have befallen this nation, unless the way had been prepared by this conflict between false opinions? Suppose the abolitionist had remained quiet; suppose he had never put forth his dogma, the *"malum in se"* theory, which, with all respect, I would say, is not to be found in the Bible; suppose he had refrained from all agitation on the subject of slavery, and just consented that the people of the Slave States, should manage their own institution, in their own way; suppose, further, that, instead of being an agitator, he had become a missionary to the South, (it was an inviting field,) and labored for the conversion of masters, conversing and mingling with them freely; endeavoring, in the spirit of that charity, inculcated in the Gospel, to convince them of their errors, whilst, at the same time, he had access to the slaves, both to preach to them, and to instruct them in Sabbath-schools--suppose these things, and we have a right to suppose them; what then?

That universal and bitter hatred, which possesses the hearts of the Southern against the Northern people, would have had no existence now—for it arose against abolitionists! The Churches had not been distracted and divided! Harmony and concord had still reigned, as in former years, from one extremity to the other of this great republic. And, above all, the process of gradual emancipation might have been going forward still, as formerly.

It was as late as the year 1808 that the African slave trade was abolished in this country. This was a triumph, which, as I must think, was achieved by christianity. Since that period, several of the States in which slavery had existed, have abolished the institution. New York became a free State as late, I believe, as the year 1827, just a short time before the ultra abolitionists began their efforts at agitation. And, at the very moment, when those efforts were commenced; and the new dogma was announced, memorials were circulating in the State of Kentucky, to which thousands of signatures had been obtained, praying the Legislature so to change the constitution, as to provide for the gradual extinction of slavery in the State. But these memorials were withdrawn in consequence of those efforts, and the work of emancipation was stopped. There has been no advance since, till this war was initiated. Emancipation is accomplished now, with a vengeance!

I confess myself among the number of those who believe, that, there is an inherent moral power in christianity, adequate to the complete regeneration of the world, and the suppression of all those evils which afflict human society. Under its benign auspices, emancipation might have pro-

gressed, till there had not been found one slave
in christendom.   The unity of the churches might
have been preserved.   The friendly relations between the inhabitants of the different sections of
the Union, might have been maintained.   And we
might have been spared the pain of witnessing
the horrors of this cruel war.   But, the Infinite
Ruler of the universe had willed otherwise, and
he raised up the instruments to execute the purpose of his will.

I will, here, take the liberty to introduce a
short extract from an article in the Princeton Review, published several years before the beginning
of our national troubles.   It is a very able and
lucid dissertation on the subject of slavery.   In
it, the author, supposed to be Dr. Hodge, plainly
forewarned the country of what would inevitably
be the consequences of a persistent effort, on the
part of abolitionists, to maintain the "*malum in
se*" theory.   What he foretold as a necessary and
logical consequence of that theory, we see, now,
to be an accomplished fact.

"The assumption that slave-holding is itself a
crime, is not only an error, but it is an error
fraught with evil consequences.   It not merely
brings its advocates into conflict with the Scrip-

tures, but it does much to retard the progress of freedom ; it embitters, and divides the members of the community, and distracts the christian church. Its operation in retarding the progress of freedom, is obvious and manifold. In the first place, it directs the battery of the enemies of slavery to the wrong point. It might be easy for them to establish the injustice or cruelty of certain slave laws, where it is not in their power to establish the sinfulness of slavery itself. They, therefore, waste their strength. Nor, is this the least evil. They promote the cause of their opponents. If they do not discriminate between slave-holding and the slave-laws, it gives the slave-holder, not merely an excuse, but an occasion, and a reason for making no such distinction. He is thus led to feel the same conviction in the propriety of the one, that he does in that of the other. His mind and conscience may be satisfied, that the mere act of holding slaves is not a crime. This is the point, however, to which the abolitionist directs his attention. He examines their arguments, and becomes convinced of their inconclusiveness, and is not only thus rendered impervious to their attacks, but is exasperated by what he considers their unmerited abuse. In the mean time, his at-

tention is withdrawn from far more important
points ; the manner in which he treats his slaves,
and the laws enacted for the security of his posession. These are points on which his judgment
might be much more readily convinced of error,
and his conscience of sin.

"Again, the opinion, that slave-holding is, itself a crime, must operate to *produce the disunion
of the States, and the division of all the ecclesiastical
societies in this country.* The feelings of the people may be excited violently for a time, but the
transport soon passes away. But if the conscience
is enlisted in the cause, and becomes the control-
ling principle, the alienation between the North
and the South, must become permanent. The opposition to Southern institutions will become calm,
constant and unappeasable. Just so far as this
opinion operates, it will lead those who entertain
it, to submit to any sacrifices to carry it out, and
give it effect. *We shall become two nations, in feeling, which must soon render us two nations in fact.*
With regard to the church, its operation will
be more summary. If slave-holding is a heinous
crime, *slave-holders must be excluded from the church.*
Several of our judicatories have already taken
this position. Should the General Assembly

adopt it, the church is, *ipso facto* divided. If the opinion in question is correct, it must be maintained, whatever are the consequences. We are no advocates of expediency in morals. We have no more right to teach error, in order to prevent evil, than we have a right to do evil, to promote good. On the other hand, if the opinion is incorrect, its evil consequences render it a duty to prove and exhibit its unsoundness. It is under the deep impression that, the primary assumption of the abolitionists is an error, that its adoption *tends to the distraction of the country, and the division* of the church; and that it will lead to the longer continuance and greater severity of slavery, that we have felt constrained to do what little we could, towards its correction."

Now, the above paragraphs, let it be remembered, were penned months and years before the logical and necessary tendency of this fundamental doctrine of the abolitionists, had been fully developed. But, being able to perceive the connection between a cause and its effects, the writer foresaw clearly, and predicted what must be the consequences of that system. And now, we have to record those consequences as accomplished facts—

in every particular, except in regard to the statement in the last sentence, where the writer says:
"it will lead to the longer continuance of slavery." It has led to the sudden and immediate
downfall of slavery in this country. But, as I
stated before, the result was decreed by the Power
that rules over all.

Henceforward, I am an abolitionist. I have
been one, from the day of the bombardment of
Fort Sumter. I was then, as well convinced that
God had purposed the immediate and utter overthrow of the institution, as I was, when President
Lincoln issued the Proclamation of Emancipation.
I will not, knowingly, be found in the ranks of
those who resist, or fight against that overruling
Providence. I am in favor of immediate and entire emancipation, and shall co-operate cordially,
and with all my energies, with abolitionists and
all others who labor for the accomplishment of
this end. Though I have ever believed that slavery is an evil, yet I do not now, and never did
accord in the sentiment, that all slavery is a sin.
But, in regard to the system of African slavery,
as it prevailed in the South, I am free to express
my opinion that it is a *system of iniquity* and a

compound of horrors. If I have not already sufficiently made known the reasons for this opinion, I shall endeavor to do so, in the subsequent pages of this work.

IX.

CHRISTIANITY VERSUS SLAVERY.

DOES Christianity sanction or tolerate slavery? It has been argued by many, who profess to be Christians, that it does, and many books have been written to prove it. But here is what the Divine Author of Christianity says; "The Spirit of the Lord is upon me, because he hath anointed me to preach the Gospel to the poor; He hath sent me to heal the broken-hearted, to preach deliverance to the captives, and recovering of sight to the blind; to set at liberty them that are bound; to preach the acceptable year of the Lord." The acceptable year of the Lord is supposed to refer to the year of jubilee, which was the year, when, under the old Jewish dispensation, all the prisoners and captives were set at liberty.

The Son of God proclaims that the words of this prophecy were to be fulfilled by his mission into the world. Now I design to show that He is acting in accordance with what he said was the design of his mission to this earth. He is freeing the captive from his chains. He is bringing liberty to them that were bound. He is so managing and directing, by his mighty Providence. the affairs of this world, as to hasten and bring about a grand jubilee to the whole earth, when all shall be free.

We know, that, before the dawn of the Christian era, slavery existed, and had existed, from time immemorial, almost throughout the world. It existed in Egypt. It existed in Persia. It existed among the Jews. It existed among the Greeks. It prevailed in the Roman Empire. It existed in nearly all the countries of modern Europe.

Not only did Turks sell christians, and white men sell black men, but white men sold slaves of their own color and race. Even our ancestors in England, sold their own brethren, of the Anglo-Saxon race, into the most ignominious bondage. These are facts, well known to every student of history. And yet, no voice, has ever been lifted up, in condemnation of the universal practice, save the voice of christianity.

But how stands the case now? Slavery has been blotted out, from every country, where the christian is the prevailing religion, except Brazil, the Spanish West Indies, and our Southern States; and in the last named, we see, that, under the effect of the stores of Divine vengeance, which have descended on the heads of those who upheld the accursed system, it is just now in the agonies of dissolution.

The selling of human beings as slaves, is no longer tolerated or practised in any of the countries of Europe. It is extremely doubtful whether the system can survive ten years longer in Cuba or Brazil. And when it shall receive its death blow there, it will cease forever to have any existence in the new world.

This is what christianity has done, and is doing, for the cause of freedom. The march of the latter, is co-extensive with the progress of the former.

Let there be none in the ranks of the church-militant, who deny to Jesus Christ, the honor of these glorious triumphs of the gospel, in favor of human liberty. Let no one be heard to make the objection, that the African slave trade was originated, and carried on, under the auspices and patronage of christian countries. Those countries were nominally christian, it is true, but, really and emphatically, they were infidel. What was France, but an infidel country? Spain was no better. And England was quite as much given up to licentiousness and free thinking, as either. Read the chronicles of those days, and you will be satisfied, that, as late as only one hundred years ago, at least nine out of ten of all the men who had any political influence or power in England, as well as in France and other countries, were open and avowed infidels.

The same thing may be said concerning the state of religious and moral sentiment, in our own country, some eighty or one hundred years ago. Men, in the highest position, were in the habit of making a boast of their infidel opinions. The writings of Tom Paine and Voltaire, were far more popular than the sacred Scriptures.

One member of Congress was known to address another member, in a letter, in which he asserted that they ought to begin to deal with preachers and priests as they were doing in France. This was while the guillotine was in operation. Another member of Congress called at a book-store in Philadelphia, to purchase a Bible. The bookseller told him that they kept no Bibles for sale. "No Bibles?"—inquiringly responded the Congress-

man — "No, sir" — returned the merchant, and
added, "we begin to think that the time is near,
when the Bible will be neither read nor sold in
Philadelphia." The statesman, who happened to
be a believer in the truth of Revelation, though
not a church member, was indignant at this remark, and administered a severe but just rebuke;
"sir, the Bible will be read and sold in Philadelphia, a thousand years after you have been roast-
ing in hell!"

I have mentioned these incidents, simply for the
purpose of conveying a faint conception of the
deplorable state of morals and religion in these
several countries, at the period, when the bloody
traffic in the bodies and souls of men, was in the
height of its glory. It may truly be said, that
the voice of christianity was silent, so far as legislation in civil affairs was concerned, during all
those years. Indeed, to attribute this cruel and
nefarious traffic to any christian influence or
power, as its origin and source, would be a libel
against God himself.

A great change has taken place in the aspect
of things, since the dawn of the present century.
Christianity is beginning to achieve her destined
triumphs, and, as soon as she gains the ascend-

ency in any country, the fetters immediately fall from the limbs of the enslaved and oppressed. To the persevering efforts of Wilberforce, Clarkson and other distinguished philanthropists and statesmen, we justly ascribe the triumph of the principles of justice and humanity, which resulted in the suppression of the African slave-trade. Few men, whose names are emblazoned in history, have done more for their race. We believe that they were divinely fitted and raised up, for the work which they accomplished. In portraying, in the British Parliament, the wrongs of bleeding humanity, we believe that it was the voice of Jesus Christ which spoke through them.

Why should slavery disappear, and retreat before the successful and triumphant progress of christianity? The answer is not obscure or difficult. It is, essentially, a system of cruelty, whereas, christianity is a system of mercy! They are antagonistic systems, and cannot, by any possibility, be combined, or made to coalesce. The most zealous advocate of African slavery, would be compelled, if he were candid, to admit that it is a system of cruelty, oppression, and murder!

Look at slavery, in its origin. It robbed Africa of forty millions of her children, who were carried in chains, and sold in distant countries. In the enslavement of these, a like number perished, who were murdered outright, or died under the barbarities inflicted by kidnappers. Is it not a system of cruelty—a very *combination of horrors*—as Thomas Jefferson called it? Can we refuse to believe that it was the purpose of Christ's mission into the world, to destroy all such iniquitous systems?

Again, look at slavery in its more matured state, and in its full-grown developments, as it has existed in our Southern States—"What are the fruits of the system during the last fifty years?" More than one hundred thousand murders, committed by blows and other injuries, inflicted by overseers and masters, for which no legal process was ever instituted—from four to five millions of men, women, and children, sold by domestic slave-traders, and carried into distant States, thus deprived of all hope of ever seeing wife, husband, children, or parents again—at least half a million of slave-children, sacrificed in infancy, whose death was caused by cruelty to their mothers, at a period when they required to be treated with tenderness and care—laws enacted, putting fetters on the mind itself, binding it down in ignorance, and debarring it from all access to that knowledge, which ought to be as free as the air we breathe —thousands of aristocratic families, reveling in luxuries and wealth, the fruits of slave-breeding, which has been a legitimate and creditable occupation in several of the States. These are some of the fruits of slavery, during the last half-century. Is it any thing else but a system of cruelty and murder? When darkness can dwell with light, or exist under the brightness of the noonday sun, then may this system of iniquity, be brought into a state of harmony with *God's system of mercy*.

The spirit of christianity breathes "*peace on earth and good will to man.*" This was the proclamation with which its birth was announced. But *good will* to universal man, cannot mean that some men, may bind others, of their fellow-men, in chains, and sell them as slaves.

The Divine Redeemer of the world, proclaimed that he came to *destroy the works of the devil, and to deliver* those who, all *their lives, were held in bondage.* But we are sure, he did not intend to teach that those whom he had delivered from the power of their master, the devil, and made the Lord's freedmen, should be held still as captives and slaves by any of the devil's confederates. Where he has lost his authority, they certainly can have no right to lord it over God's children.

The very essence of christianity is love—love to God and love for man. "Love is the fulfilling of the law." "Thou shalt love thy neighbor, as thyself." "By this shall ye know that ye are my disciples, that ye love one another." "If any man say that he loves God, whom he hath not seen, and hateth his brother, whom he hath seen, he is a liar."

All the disciples of Christ, are called brethren. Can a man love his brother as himself, and yet claim the right to sell him—to sell his wife and children—to cut and-mark his body with stripes —to deprive him of all means of knowledge—to exact his toil with sweat and stripes and allow him no wages! Is this what is meant by the new command Christ gave to his disciples, to love one another?

But this question is not a novel one. Very soon after the introduction of African slavery into this country, the question arose, whether christianity does not enfranchise its converts. "The Christian world"—I now quote from Bancroft's History—"The christian world of that day, almost

universally, revered in Christ, the impersonation
of the Divine wisdom.   Could an intelligent being,
who, through the Mediator, had participated in the
Spirit of God, and, by his own inward experience,
had.become conscious of a supreme existence, and
of relations between that existence and humanity
be rightfully held in bondage ?   From New England to Carolina, the notion prevailed, that, 'being
baptized is inconsistent with a state of slavery ;'
and this early apprehension proved a main obstacle to the culture and conversion of these poor
people.   The sentiment was so deep and general,
that South Carolina, in 1712, Maryland in 1715,
Virginia repeatedly, from 1667 to 1748, gave a
negative to it by special enactments."

This is, certainly, a very curious and instructive
passage of history.   What was the notion which
prevailed "from New England to Carolina," and
was " so *deep and general*," as to cause masters to
deprive their slaves of all means of religious instruction and conversion, lest they should lose
their right of ownership in them?   It was the
notion, that, if they should be converted, and received into the Church by the holy ordinance of
baptism, they could no longer be rightfully held
in a state of slavery.   Under the influence of this

general and deep religious conviction, the conversion of a slave, if he belonged to a Christian
master, necessarily secured his manumission.

From what source, did the Christians of that
early day, obtain this deep and almost universal
religious impression? Let the modern advocates
of slavery, who claim, to belong to the Christian brotherhood, answer.

But the prevalence of this sentiment, was an
obstacle in the way of the religious instruction
and conversion of the poor slaves. For, as, in
the case of a majority of the planters, their cupidity and avarice preponderated over their religious
convictions, they adopted measures to keep these
Africans in ignorance, and to prevent their conversion, lest they should lose their right of property in them, as slaves. The State legislatures
had to take up the subject, and enact special laws,
urging and enforcing on masters the observance
of those duties, in the treatment of their slaves,
which every dictate of reason, as well as religion,
required. But these enactments failed to have
the desired effect, as the love of lucre was stronger
than piety in the hearts of the masters, and they
were not willing to let their slaves be converted,
till the legislatures had solemnly declared, by a

legislative act, that a converted and baptized slave, might be lawfully and consistently held in a state of bondage.   But, so strong and deep was the general religious conviction to the contrary of this, that one single legislative decision was not sufficient.   The enactment had to be repeated again and again, and by different legislatures, before the conscience of those Christian masters had become schooled up to the point of permitting them, to keep and hold a Christian brother or sister as a slave.

This, to say the least, was rather an anomalous proceeding ; politicians, worldly-minded and selfish men, many of whom were, doubtless, infidels, meeting in solemn deliberation, to settle a point in religious morals ; and, by a legislative enactment, declaring that to be right and moral, which Christians generally, on their understanding of what Christ had enacted in his word, had believed to be wrong.

But they settled the question.   And this fact in history, is to be remembered by the advocates of slavery.   The Assembly of South Carolina, and other assemblies, mere secular bodies, who had no authority to legislate in matters of religious faith, established the morality of holding a Christian man or woman in bondage, in opposition to the universal sentiment of the Church in those days.

And now, let us see what the Apostle Paul has said and written on this identical subject, the holding of christian brethren in a state of slavery.

"Masters, give unto your servants, that which is just and equal, knowing that ye, also, have a master in Heaven."

Here is a law, an enactment, ordained by the highest authority, which, if universally observed, would lead to universal emancipation, in every country where christian law prevails. The duty of the master is stated, with the motive to its performance. Give to your servants, *that which justice and equity require.* This is the duty, stated in terms so clear, as not to be misunderstood, except wilfully. And the motive to the performance of this duty, is, the knowledge the master has, that he is himself a servant—that Christ is his Master, and he must, therefore, do unto his servant as he would have Christ his master in Heaven, do unto him.

Under the operation of such a law as this, no service rendered, could be without its just reward. It would insure to the slave all the education and training essential to his happiness in this world, and his preparation for another. It would afford a sure guarantee against being forcibly separated from his wife—against having his children sold, or being sold himself to some merciless tyrant. In short, such a law, if generally observed, would abolish slavery throughout the world.

Admit that there are precepts which seem to sanction slavery, as one of the institutions existing at the time, when christianity was born. They sanction it, only in such a negative manner, as to prohibit christians from putting themselves in array against existing governments, and such political and social institutions as had originated under those governments.

"Let as many servants, as are under the yoke, count their own masters worthy of all honor." Why is this precept given? The reason is immediately annexed—"that the name of God and his doctrine be not blasphemed,"—that is to say, that the heathen powers that rule be not provoked to deny Christ and to make war upon the infant church.

We know, that, if the apostles had put themselves in opposition to the civil or political institutions of their day; if, for example, they had commanded masters to liberate their slaves on the ground that all slavery is a sin; or, if they had exhorted servants to desert their masters, for the reason that they had no right to hold them in bondage, every political power of that age, and the whole heathen world would have conspired for the destruction of the church. Therefore, submission was inculcated, even to the enforcement of unjust and unrighteous laws. Hear the great apostle once more;

"Submit yourselves to every ordinance of man, for the Lord's sake. For so is the will of God, that with well-doing, ye may put to silence, the ignorance of foolish men; as free, and not using your liberty for a cloak of maliciousness, but as the servants of God. Honor all men. Love the brotherhood. Fear God. Honor the king. Servants, be subject to your masters with all fear, not only to the good and gentle, but also to the froward. For this is thank-worthy, if a man for conscience toward God, endure grief, suffering wrongfully."

Have the advocates of opposition, pondered these significant words? "It is thank-worthy"— that is, it is commendable, that a Christian, who is, at the same time, a slave, "*endure grief, suffering wrongfully*" for conscience towards God; or, because God requires him, in the present emergency, to be patient, and submit to every ordinance of man. Does such language imply any approbation of the system of wrong, under which the slave thus endures grief, and pines away in useless sighs for freedom?

The Apostle Paul assumed the responsibility of emancipating a slave, who belonged not to himself, but to another. Perhaps this statement is rather too strong; and I qualify it, by saying, that he wrote such a letter to Philemon, in behalf of Onesimus, that it had been impossible for Philemon longer to have kept him in involuntary servitude. I will quote the passage entire:

"Wherefore, though I might be much bold in Christ, to inform thee that which is convenient, yet, for love's sake, I rather beseech thee, being such a one as Paul the aged, and now also a prisoner of Jesus Christ. I beseech thee for my son Onesimus, whom I have begotten in my bonds, which in time past, was to thee unprofitable, but now, profitable to thee and to me; whom I have sent again; thou therefore receive him, that is, mine own bowels; whom I would have retained with me, that, in thy stead, he might have ministered unto me in the bonds of

the Gospel; but without thy mind, would I do
nothing, that thy benefit should not be, as it
were, of necessity, but willingly. For, perhaps,
he therefore departed for a season, that thou
shouldst receive · him forever; not now as a
servant, but above a servant, a brother beloved,
especially to me, but how much more unto thee,
both in the flesh, and in the Lord? If thou
count me, therefore, a partner, receive him as myself. If he hath wronged thee, or oweth aught,
put that on mine account; I Paul have written
it with mine own hand, I will repay it; albeit
I do not say to thee, how thou owest unto me
even thine own self besides. Yea, brother, let
me have joy of thee in the Lord; refresh my
bowels in the Lord. Having confidence in thy
obedience, I wrote unto thee, knowing that thou
wilt also do more than I say."

What a tender and loving appeal is this whole
letter—though he might have used the language
of command, yet, for love's sake, he chose to employ the language of entreaty, in behalf of Onesimus—I *beseech thee* for *my son Onesimus.* He
speaks of him as *his son,* his *own bowels*—and
exhorts Philemon to *receive* him as himself, that
is, with all the marks of esteem and brotherly

love, with which he would have received the great Apostle. He exhorts him, to receive him, *not as a slave*, or servant, but *above a servant*—as *a brother beloved*, both *in the flesh*, and *in the Lord*. Does not this imply a command to Philemon, to liberate his slave, to set Onesimus free, since he is now *a brother beloved in the Lord ?*

He intimates that he would have retained Onesimus with him, as he had a right, but he sends him back, not to be a slave again, but that he, Philemon, might perform the favor or benefit which he solicited, *willingly*, or voluntarily, and not from *necessity* or constraint.

Paul knew that Philemon would do what he requested—"*having confidence in thy obedience*, I wrote unto thee, *knowing that thou wilt also do more than I say.*"

And what was the result? Onesimus was emancipated. He was never held in bondage another day. And we may believe that a brother in Christ, so highly commended as Philemon, regarded as an occasion for devout gratitude, the privilege of performing an act of kindness, at once so just and so consonant to the Spirit of Christ.

We afterwards find Onesimus as a fellow-laborer

with Paul, in the bonds of the Gospel, and employed by him as a messenger to the churches. Ho finally settled at Ephesus, and became its bishop as we are informed by St. Ignatius, and his memory is cherished by many, as one of the martyrs of the church.

Now, in this case, I confess that I see an *act of emancipation*, based solely on the ground, that the enslaved had become, *spiritually*, the son, and therefore the equal of Paul himself—had become the brother, and therefore the equal of Philemon the master, and *beloved in the Lord*. It was on this ground alone, that his freedom was solicited, and that it was granted.

The case may, or may not, furnish a general rule or principle, which may apply to all similar cases. I undertake not to determine. But I may be allowed to say that I feel truly grateful that though I have lived so many years in the midst of the evils of slavery, I have never claimed the right of *ownership* or *property*, in one of Christ's brethren.

X.

THE VOICE OF BLOOD.

MURDER is a crime that never goes unpunished! We may not know what mark was branded on the first murderer, Cain; but we do know the malediction of the Most High fell on him, and he became a fugitive and a vagabond in the earth. And, doubtless, the complaint which fell from his lips, "*my punishment is greater than I can bear*," has found an echo, in the heart of every one, who in any age or country since, has imbrued his hands in the blood of a fellow-being.

Let the murderer go where he will, he feels that he is but a fugitive and a vagabond. The anger of God has burned his guilt deep into his conscience.

He may escape the penalty affixed to his crime by the laws of the land. He may conceal his crime from the knowledge of men, but he cannot hide it from himself, nor from the all-seeing

eye of his Maker. Wherever he goes, in whatever
country he may seek to be unknown, the curse
goes with him, the voice of his brother's blood
seeming, every where, to rise out of the very
ground, on which he treads, and crying for vengeance. He may shift from one scene of revelry
and merriment, to another, to drown thought.
But 'tis all in vain; he is not, and he cannot be,
a happy man. The curse of the Almighty is rest-
ing on him. The uneasy and anxious countenance, and the restless eye, betray a soul ill at
ease.

O, have you ever known one who had the guilt
of murder on his conscience! He can hardly trust
himself alone, and yet, he seems as if he would
avoid all intercourse with his fellow-men. He is
afraid his dreadful secret will be disclosed, and
yet, it is with difficulty, he can keep from betray-
ing that secret himself. He bears in his own
bosom, the punishment of his crime, which he
would fain expiate on the scaffold, if only he
dared to brave public sentiment, and bring disgrace on his family by letting the world know,
that he bears the mark of Cain on his forehead.
Yea, the curse of the Almighty pursues the murderer!

No decree can be more just than that which was long ago enacted; "Whoso sheddeth man's blood, by man shall his blood be shed." Not only does the felon, who deprives another of existence, take away that which he cannot restore, but, if we can understand the inspired declaration —" for *in the image of God created he him*"—he mars that Divine image, as originally impressed on the soul of man. And from the connection in which that declaration stands recorded, we may fairly infer that there is no crime which transcends this.

I acknowledge, I am one of those who believe that "*no murderer hath eternal life abiding in him.*" It may be wrong, but still, I cannot banish from my mind the doubt, whether one, who has, deliberately, and with malice aforethought, stained his soul with the crime of murder, can be pardoned, either in this world, or the next. "He has not only deprived his victim of life, but, it may be, has sent that victim, unprepared, to the doom of a miserable eternity! And it revolts our sense of justice, to suppose that he is pardoned, and enjoys the favor of God, through a blissful eternity, while his victim is suffering the vengeance of God.

I have been with a condemned criminal, in
his prison. I knew that he had a murderer's
heart. Moved by the spirit of revenge, he had
sought his victim, and, at the dark hour of midnight, had deliberately shot him through the heart.
I did not feel prompted by a sense of Christian duty, to kneel down and offer up a prayer
for his pardon. The conviction was so strong
in my mind, that there could be no pardon for
him, that I dared not do it. And I left the cell,
without even making the attempt. I may have
been wrong, but I could not resist my convictions,
nor act contrary to them. I had known the victim of his revenge, and had reason to believe,
that, though a better man than the murderer, he
was quite unprepared for his sudden and unex-
pected exit to worlds unknown.

I have said that African slavery was a system
of wholesale murder. At whose hand, is the
blood of the millions slain by it, now required?
The *Decree of Justice*, against the crime of murder,
has never been repealed. And the Eternal, we
may be sure, will take care for the inviolability of
His own law. The execution of that law may be
sometimes, and often is, long delayed, yet the
wicked shall not, for that reason, go unpunished.

Retributive justice must, soon or late, overtake the guilty.

In the book of God's remembrance, the system of African slavery, is charged with the guilt of the murder of many millions of his children, formed originally in his own image. Rigid justice demands an atonement. And, unless the Decree, quoted above, has been repealed, an atonement will be exacted in blood. And because this shed blood has been crying so long unavenged, must we suppose, either that God does not hear, or that he will not attend to that cry at last?

Historical writers have told us, that, for the forty millions of the inhabitants of Africa, torn from their native country, and made slaves in America, an equal number were cruelly put to death, in various ways, by those emissaries of hell, who were employed in the infernal trade. Will there be no final reckoning for this?—no party, who will be held accountable at the bar of the Great Judge, for this lavish waste of human life?

And here, it may be proper to note this striking and essential difference between African slavery, and every other form of slavery ever known in the world. Can we suppose, that, even Abraham would have been guiltless in the sight of

God, if he had imported his slaves thousands of
miles, from another continent, in dark and sus-
picious looking vessels, manned by pirates, at a
cost of, at least, one murder committed for every
slave obtained? Would the ancient Hebrews
have been sinless, in the matter of slavery, if they
had been guilty of the same nefarious practice?
Their bondmen were natives of the soil. But yet,
the Jews made no attempt to enslave them, till
they had received an *express command* from their
Divine Legislator, to do so. Even the heathen
nations, of the Roman Empire, who held slaves,
had at least the shadow of justice in the title, by
which they held them; as they had been taken as
captives in the wars with neighboring States, or
had been sold to them for debt. In short, this
system of modern slavery, considered simply with
reference to its origin, is as much blacker than
those ancient forms of bondage, as the age of
christianity, exceeds in brightness, the ages of
darkness, when those ancient forms of slavery prevailed.

The question still recurs, who will be-held to a
rigid account, for all this bloodshed? Suppose
that they were tender and helpless babes, whose
brains were dashed out against the trunk of a

tree—Suppose that they were aged and infirm
men and women, valueless as slaves, and unable
to endure the fatigues of the march to the coast,
who were therefore shot down, or stabbed, and
left weltering in their blood—Suppose that others
were consumed in the fire of their own dwellings—
Suppose that many perished, from fatigue and exhaustion, in the hurried march, naked and barefoot, over burning sands, to the coast—Suppose
that many more died of a broken heart, or of fever
and other diseases contracted from the foul and
pestilential air, in the confined hold of the ship—
or, suppose that, sick and dying, they were thrown
overboard, to feed the sharks ; who is responsible
for so many millions of murders, committed under
the full blaze and light of the sun of heaven ?

It avails naught, to say that nobody will be
held responsible. Nor, is it a satisfactory answer, to say, that the guilt belongs solely to the
kidnappers, or the persons immediately engaged in
the slave-trade. What were they, but the mere
instruments or agents of others? Would they
have robbed Africa, if there had not been a
market for the spoils? The people who kept
that market open, were the people who tempted
the kidnappers to engage in the traffic—who

paid them for it—and, in fact, employed them as their agents, while thus carrying on a trade, marked, at every step, by rapine and bloodshed!

If the colonies of Virginia and the Carolinas had acted as did the colony of Georgia, under Oglethorpe's administration,—or as did the people of New England, when the first cargo of Africans was landed on their coast; who raised such a cry of indignation, against the owners of the ship, that they were arrested as malefactors and murderers, and the cargo of slaves were sent back to their native country, at the public expense. If those colonies had acted in this spirit, and persisted in such a course, there would have been no slavery in this country. The kidnappers would have had no patrons, and for the want of patronage, would have been compelled to betake themselves to some useful occupation.

Those colonists must have known what they were doing, when they *created the slave market*, and threw its doors wide open, inviting the kidnappers to enter upon their hellish trade. They knew that every slave imported was the purchase of blood and crime. They knew that every slaveship which arrived on the coast, had buried its scores of murdered victims, in the depths of the ocean. They were not ignorant of the cruelties and horrors of the slave-trade.

We are driven, therefore, to the conclusion, that the states which *kept the market*, and encouraged and rewarded the kidnappers, while carrying on the diabolical traffic, are, really, the guilty and responsible parties.

It is now two hundred and forty-three years, since the first cargo of slaves was landed on our shores. And what does the history of the peculiar institution exhibit, as it has existed in these states, during that period? I do not exaggerate, when I say, that the blood of not less than two hundred thousand slaves, is crying to heaven for vengeance, from this soil of freedom, whose death was caused by blows and wounds inflicted, in the severity of punishment, by the inhumanity of masters and overseers. There has been *no reckoning, no atonement*. The law of man did not even demand a legal investigation. Their life was crushed out of them, by a crime, but no notice was taken thereof. May we suppose, or can we believe that the Divine Legislator, will, in like manner, ignore the existence of his law against crime, and pass by this numerous class of offenders and murderers, without the least notice. Will

He also turn a deaf ear to those unavailing cries
for mercy, which those murdered slaves poured
in vain in the ears of the tyrants, when sinking
under the hand of violence, into death?

No! His law is perfect, and so rigidly just, that,
not the slightest infraction thereof, can go unno-
ticed! We believe this—we must believe it, if we
believe in His existence at all!

About the year 1832, I spent a few months
in Greene County, in the State of Alabama.
It was the first year of my residence in the
Slave States. In the immediate neighborhood,
where I sojourned, there was a lady, the wife
of a planter, who beat a young servant girl,
aged about twelve years, in such a cruel manner, as to cause her death. She had struck her
a number of times with a heavy stick, or blud-
geon, and, perhaps, in a state of excitement and
anger, inflicted blows of such a nature, as that she
died soon after. But no notice was ever taken
of the matter, further than to cause a little talk
in the immediate neighborhood, at the time.

I knew a wealthy planter, who resided in another State, some years ago. He was a native
Southron, who had led a very dissolute and in-
temperate life. On one occasion, as if in sheer

sport, he caught up one of his negro children by the feet, and swinging it around violently, in the air, dashed its head against a horse-block, in the yard, so that the blood spurted from its nostrils and mouth, causing its death, almost instantaneously. The body was buried, of course ; and, if it had a soul, as I presume it had, it passed away to eternity and to God, and, for aught we know to the contrary, was permitted to rehearse to the Universal Father, the circumstances by which it was so unceremoniously hurried home. But no charge was ever preferred against the planter. No jury was impanneled to try his case. No legal action whatever was ever taken. He was a wealthy man, and the child was his own property.

Another wealthy planter, on the coast, not far from New Orleans, was tried by a court, for the murder of a slave, one of his own, a small boy, six or seven years old. But he had money, and he was easily acquitted. To punish one of his female domestics, a handsome mulatto woman, for her obstinacy in not yielding to his unlawful desires, he put her little son in the bake-oven, and caused it to be heated to such a degree, that he lived but a few minutes, after being extricated.

That planter is still living ; but as he is a rebel, and has gone beyond the lines, into the Confederacy, I presume his large property has been, or will be confiscated.

A soldier in the regiment, with which I am connected, relates that he has been twice captured, as a runaway, by bloodhounds. I am not aware that any law has ever been enacted, in any Slave State, to put a stop to this savage practice. There are men who keep hounds, and make a business of catching runaways, and are paid so much per head. The same soldier mentions the case of a slave he knew, who was so lacerated and torn by these ferocious animals, before the owners could come up with them, that he actually died. He himself escaped the same horrible fate, only by ascending into a tree, when he found that he was about to be caught. Perhaps this was not strictly a case of murder, as the killing was done by the bloodhounds. But will the Author of life hold the bloodhounds responsible, for the loss of life in such a case, instead of the owners? Or can the State be considered as guiltless, that tolerates and allows of such a practice?

I might easily fill up a volume, by detailing incidents and facts of this kind. But this is not my design, although I would do so, if I considered it necessary to aid the cause of humanity, giving facts and dates, with the names of parties and witnesses. But my purpose has been simply to show that the lives of slaves have been almost absolutely at the disposal of their owners, and the merciless task-masters who had charge of them, and that the State legislatures have not afforded them that protection, to which, as subjects of God's Government, and a part of the great family of man, they were entitled.

The miserable tyrants are aware of this. They know that the African slaves have not been dealt with, as if they were *men*. And, therefore, they have adopted a theory in accordance with their practice. They affect to believe that they are an inferior race of beings, altogether different from the white or European race, and not many degrees removed from the baboon tribes, and to be, accordingly, treated as other irrational animals. This theory was designed as an apology and excuse for their inhumanity to their slaves.

The day of retribution has come at last! The innocent blood that has been shed in this land, has not cried so long to Heaven for vengeance, in vain!

XI.

RACHEL'S LAMENTATION.

HARK! what voice was that, heard in Rama?
"The voice of lamentation, and weeping, and
great mourning, Rachel weeping for her children,
and would not be comforted, because they are
not."

Herod, that monster of iniquity, than whom a
more cruel tyrant never sat on a throne, finding
that he had been mocked of the wise men, who
came from the East to worship the Infant Jesus,
issued a decree that all the children of Bethle-
hem, and the coasts round about, should be put to
death. Under this bloody edict, some hundreds,
perhaps several thousands of tender and helpless
babes, were torn from their mothers' embrace,
and cruelly slaughtered.

The intention of the decree, was, to cut off the
infant Saviour, whose advent to the world had
been proclaimed by angels. I presume not to

decide what share this event may have had in the
fearful retribution which fell upon the guilty city
and capital of the nation, from which that edict
was issued, seventy years afterwards. But history
tells us that more than a million of the inhabitants perished miserably, who were put to the
sword, or died of famine. During the siege, delicate females fed on the flesh of their own babes,
to appease the gnawings of their hunger.

There is another similar record in history, still
more ancient, of the wholesale slaughter of young
children, with the retribution which followed, but
stated in such terms as to leave no doubt as to
the connection between the crime and the punishment.

The king of Egypt, in order to prevent the too
rapid increase of the Hebrews, ordered that all
their male children, should be strangled at their
birth. How just and striking was the retribution,
that was visited on the whole land of Egypt!
The Lord sent a destroying angel, which passed
over the land, and slew the first-born in every house
of the Egyptians, from the first-born of the king
that was heir to the throne, to the first-born of
the humblest peasant. *Here was blood for blood !*

If the slave-holders in this country, had not,

every year, destroyed the infant children of their
slaves, thereby preventing their rapid increase, the
Africans, would, long ago, have been the ruling
power in America. The forty millions transported
from Africa, and brought hither, would certainly
have outnumbered, two to one, the whole number
of Europeans who have emigrated to this continent. They are known to be a prolific race, and
I see no reason, why the forty millions should not
have doubled, at least once, in the course of two
or three centuries which would have given a population of eighty millions at the present time. But
instead of this number, there are not over ten
millions of Africans in all America. Where are
the seventy millions? What is the cause of this
extraordinary decrease?

I affirm that a system of infanticide has prevailed, by which their infants have been annually
offered up, by tens of thousands, as victims on the
altar of the slave-god!

I know that this is a grave charge, to bring
against slave-holders, and the states that have upheld and supported the institution. But I make
the charge under a full sense of my responsibility,
and proceed to the proof.

Every one, who knows any thing of the statistics of slavery, is aware that in every country, in which it has prevailed, the number of deaths have exceeded the number of births, among the slave-population, except, perhaps, the United States. M. Cochin, a French author, asserts, that "it is a law of nature, that, in all slave countries, the deaths exceed the births." This is a fact, well established, both by official documents and foreign statistics.

At Surinam, from 1839 to 1843, a period of four years, five thousand nine hundred slaves were born, whilst there were ten thousand four hundred who died, or nearly two to one, during the same period.

In the year 1825, the slave-population of Cuba, amounted to two hundred and fifty-six thousand. But if we accept the calculation of Baron Humboldt, the whole number of slaves, which had been imported into the island from Africa, from the beginning of the slave-trade was four hundred thirteen thousand five-hundred, so that the number of deaths, during that period, exceeded the births by one hundred and fifty-seven thousand five hundred. Any country would soon be without an inhabitant, at this rate of depopulation.

It is computed, that, during the last century,

six hundred thousand slaves were imported into Jamaica, yet it is known, that, at the end of that century, the slave-population of the whole island, amounted to but little more than half the number. The deaths exceeded the births by nearly three hundred thousand.

If a census had been taken annually, in our own Southern States, showing, not only the increase in population, white and black, but how many slaves had been introduced into each state by importation, I would be able to prove, that, for the past forty years, in the States of Alabama, Mississippi, Louisiana and Arkansas, the deaths, among the slaves, have exceeded the births, by at least one-third.

Now, what is the cause of this extraordinary mortality? This is no insignificant inquiry.—It demands our most serious consideration.—The great Judge Himself will require an answer, in the Day of final Reckoning—*What is the cause?* For nothing can be more certain, than that there is a cause.

There is a natural and original law of increase, by which the populations of states and countries, are increased in a steady ratio. That law was established when God said to the seed

of Adam, "Be fruitful, and multiply, and replenish the earth." That law is never suspended or
relaxed by any natural cause.

We see that the African race is prolific and
fruitful, in their own native country. We see
that, in every kingdom and state of Europe, the
population is steadily advancing in numbers, notwithstanding the loss of so many thousands, by
emigration to other countries. We observe how
rapidly the white race is multiplying in the several divisions of America. I repeat it, that original law of our Maker, is never reversed nor
suspended by natural causes. What is the un-
natural cause, which has reversed it, in the case
of the slave-population in this country? What
is it which has killed so many millions of human
beings, and sent them, prematurely, from time into
eternity? There is a cause—O my God! thou
knowest what it is!

It cannot be ascribed to the influence of climate. For, how often have slave-holders themselves said that the sultry regions of the South
belong to the slave—that it is the climate most
congenial and adapted to his nature. One of
their principal arguments in defense of slavery,
is founded on this assumption. They assert that

this fair and sunny realm of the South, so rich
and productive, must be cultivated by the labor
of negroes, as the white man cannot live here,
and labor. It cannot, therefore, be pretended,
that this extraordinary mortality is the effect of
climate. The climate is more fatal to the white
race than to the blacks; yet everywhere, even in
the South, the whites have increased in population.

The cause is not, that, as a race, they have
lost their virility, or power to propagate, and are
hence beginning to decay and die out. For it
has ever been contended that there is not, on
the face of the earth, a more prolific people, or
a generation that multiplies faster. The testimony, on this point, is unanimous. A distinguished judge, in the Georgia Legislature, said
several years ago, in a speech:

"You may take any single slave-holding county
in the Southern states, in which the great staples
of cotton and sugar are cultivated to any extent,
and confine the present slave-population within
the limits of that county. Such is the *rapid
natural increase* of the slaves, and the rapid exhaustion of the soil in the cultivation of those
crops (which add so much to the commercial
wealth of the country) that, in a few years, it

would be impossible to support them within the limits of such county."

Look at the single fact, that, during the last fifteen or twenty years, the great State of Virginia has been able to supply not less than twenty-five or thirty thousand slaves annually, for the market in the cotton and sugar growing regions of the South, and yet there has been no diminution of her slave-population at home, but a regular and constant increase all the while. Do such facts seem to indicate that they are a feeble and decaying race?

If then, they have increased and multiplied rapidly in their own native land; if, in the State of Virginia, where slavery exists in its mildest form, and its rigors are not known, the race has been obedient to the great law of nature, originally given to man for the propagation of the species, what cause has interrupted the natural order of things, causing their decrease in Louisiana, Mississippi, Jamaica, Barbadoes, and other countries, where slavery has prevailed, in its more rigid forms? I will here quote a short extract from the works of the celebrated Dr. Samuel Cartwright, one of the most enthusiastic admirers and defenders of Southern slavery, who ever raised a pen in defense of it. Indeed he had become so wedded to the system, and blinded by his prejudices in favor of it, that he could hardly see any thing else but arguments in favor of it, and the inferiority of the negro race, in any book or subject that he studied. His recent death in the rebel army, raised for the purpose of battling for the institution, proves, at least, the sincerity of his zeal in the cause. The quotation is as follows :

"Nature is no law unto them. They let their children suffer and die, or unmercifully abuse them, unless the white man or woman prescribe rules in the nursery for them to go by." But why should nature be no law unto them ? Are there white females in Africa, where they do multiply, to prescribe rules in the nursery for them to go by ? Even the she wolf, and every other creature has been endowed wilh an instinctive affection for its own young. And does the writer pretend to give a single fact to prove that the negro mother is the only exception to this universal law ? But further, he says :

"Whenever the white woman superintends the nursery, whether the climate be cold or hot, *They increase faster than any other people on the face of the globe*; but, *on large plantations*, remote from her influence, the negro *population invariably diminishes*, unless the overseer take upon himself those duties, in the lying in and nursery department, which, on small estates, are attended to by the mistress. She often sits up at night with sick children, and administers to their wants, when their own mothers are nodding by them, and would he sound asleep, if it were not for her presence. The care that white women bestow on the nursery, is one of the principal causes, why three hundred thousand Africans, originally imported into the territory of the United States, have increased to four millions; while, in the British West Indies, the number imported, exceeded, by several millions, the actual population. It is also the cause, why the small proprietors of negro property in Maryland, Virginia, Kentucky and Missouri, are able to supply the loss, on the Southern plantations, which are cut off from the happy influence of the presiding genious over civilization, morality and population—the white woman."

Now, this brief extract, contains two or three admissions, inadvertently made by the writer, which go far to account for the rapid decrease of the slave-population in certain States and countries.

In the first place, it is admitted that, if the nursery is properly attended to, the race does increase, whether the climate be hot or cold, "faster than any other people on the face of the globe."

Secondly, that, if the nursery is neglected, as in the British West Indies, and on large Southern plantations, there is a rapid decrease of the population.

Thirdly, that there is, every year, a loss on the large plantations in the South, owing to this cause, and that this loss is constantly supplied by fresh importations from the more Northern Slave States, where the business is followed of breeding slaves to supply this waste of life.

I agree with this earnest and bigoted zealot for slavery, as to the cause of this destruction of human life, viz.; the absence of that tender care and influence over the nursery, without which the human offspring is not, and cannot be reared to maturity. But I cannot agree with him, in assigning to the white woman, the sphere which the Creator has given the African mother, in nursing and rearing her own child. No one can properly supply the place, to the helpless infant, of its own natural mother, notwithstanding what the writer só grandiloquently says about the happy influence of the white woman, as "the *presiding genius*, over civilization, morality and population."

That *the slave mother is, tyrannically and cruelly, denied the privilege of acting the part of a nurse to her young and delicate babe, on the large plantations,* is what I shall now endeavor to establish.

It is not true that she is wanting in natural affection for her offspring. But she has to be in the field, with the other hands, under the overseer, almost up to the very moment when she becomes a mother. And then again, by the time her babe is three weeks old, she has to resume her place among the field-hands, and work with the rest of the gang, without any interval or respite, except what is allowed her, about twice in the day, to return to the quarters to give her infant the breast. Has she any chance, under such circumstances, to discharge the duties of maternity? Does she receive the tenderness and care her own delicate situation demands? Is there any probability that a young and tender babe can grow up to maturity, with so little nursing and attention?

I have heard the remark made, in these States,

a hundred times, if not oftener, that it is almost impossible to bring up young negroes, on the larger plantations, which are left exclusively to the management of overseers. And I know the remark to be true, for I have lived many years in these States, and have been much on large plantations in Mississippi, in Louisiana, and in Texas; and I can tell the reasons why the remark is true.

These large plantations belong to men of wealth. They are located, generally, along the margins of rivers and bayous, and in the rich and alluvial districts, once covered by swamps. There are proprietors who own two, three, five, and often as many as six or eight of these large plantations each, but they do not reside on them with their families. They live in Mobile, or Montgomery, or Nashville, or Natchez, or some other gay metropolis, where aristocracy can be seen in all its pomp. The plantations, from whence they derive the means of spending their days in splendid idleness and pleasure, are left solely to the management of overseers.

The business of overseeing, has been at the South, a regular and established trade or calling, as much so as that of the lawyer, the physician, or any other established vocation. The overseer

must, of course, have a reputation for proficiency
in the business for which he is engaged. And his
reputation depends on his ability to obtain, from
the slaves under his management, the largest
amount of labor possible! The test of this, is the
number of bales of cotton or hogsheads of sugar
he can make in a season, to the hand. There is
no overseer, who is willing to be surpassed, in this
respect, by the neighboring overseers. Hence,
there is a rivalry among them, every season, who
shall raise the highest number of hogsheads or
bales, for the force employed. Will they be spar-
ing in the use of the lash? Can we suppose that
they would not begin the labor of the day, early
in the morning, or that they would not leave off
late in the evening? Seldom does the plantation
bell ring the signal for turning out for the toils
of the day, after the first dawn of light, often an
hour sooner; and the labor is continued till dark,
and frequently till nine or ten o'clock in the night.
Is it probable that the overseer would be likely,
under such circumstances, to have much regard
or sympathy for a female slave, in a delicate situation? She would scarcely dare to complain to
him, and if she did, perhaps, she would only be
driven away to her work, with a kick or a blow,

by which the womb becomes the grave of her un-
born child!

A regular finished overseer, is one who has not
in his heart, a particle of feeling or humanity for
a negro. This assertion is based on what I have,
myself, seen and observed everywhere in the
South. The whip is the badge of their profession
and the symbol of their office. They have used it
so long, and excoriated the backs of so many sup-
pliant men and women, that it is no marvel they
have become callous, and lost the capacity to feel
for one who has a dark skin. It is no unusual
thing, when these overseers are together, to hear
them boast of their new and improved modes of
torture and punishment, for runaways, and other
delinquents. In brief; I do affirm that there is
not a humane person, in the free States, who would
not entertain a supreme loathing for the wretch,
who should manifest as little compassion for his
dumb ox or his horse, as the majority of these
overseers entertain for the negro.

And now, what may be supposed to be the state
of things, on the large plantations, left solely to
the management of these men? The proprietor,
with his family, is a hundred, it may be, a thousand miles away; and on the plantation, contain-

ing a population, varying from one to five hundred human beings, there is not a white person, save the overseer. Over that population, he is an absolute despot, and rules with a rod of iron. They fear him as a tyrant. His word is law to them, and from his decision there is no appeal— not to the law of the land, of course—not even to their own master, for any wrong or outrage he may inflict. O, it is sad to think, that such a state of things should exist in a free country— should exist in this land of boasted light and liberty! But it has existed long, nevertheless.

Contemplate, for a moment, this petty tyrant, the overseer, in the exercise of the unbounded authority committed to him. He knows by what tenure he holds his office, and on what the next year's salary and employment will depend. The main purpose, therefore, by which he is actuated, is, to get as much work done as possible, without a moment's thought for the comfort or welfare, of the miserable slaves. They are divided into two or three gangs, and a driver, with whip in hand, is stationed to watch each gang. No one is permitted to lag behind, or to look up from his work. They are driven from daylight till after dark. The females *enceinte*, and the mothers *with suckling babes*, are put in the gangs, and worked with the rest. Is it not a system of infanticide? Ought it to be considered as a matter of surprise that it has been so often remarked, it is impossible to raise slave children on the large plantations!

In the cotton picking season, they are out in the morning, often in the cold dews, when there is not a dry rag of clothing on them, till the hot sun comes out towards noon, and dries it.

At Christmas time, it is usual, after the year's crop has been gathered and disposed of, to clear up and open a new field out of the swamp, and get it ready for planting, in the coming spring. This is the wet season of the year in the South. No matter if it blows rain and sleet, a week at a time—no matter if the ground is covered with water, ankle or knee deep—the work must go on, for it has to be finished within a given time. During the planting season, there is no time to clear a new field, and it must be done in the interval between the gathering of one crop, and the planting of another. And this is the winter season, the most inclement of the year, when no white man would think of going into the swamp or marshes, and chopping timber for weeks together, in the water and rain. He would choose the summer season for the purpose, when the sun has dried the earth, and there is no exposure, consequently, of life and health. But this is the busiest - season of the year, when the slaves are in the crop, and cannot be spared for clearing new lands. This fact may serve to throw light on the mysterious cause of negro consumption, so prevalent in some districts, and also, explain why it is, that, on nearly every large plantation, there may be found, at any time, a number of the helpless. and hopeless victims of rheumatism, unable to walk or drag their slow limbs along, who must just linger on a few more miserable days, and then die. The women go into the swamp, and chop and clear away the timber, the same as the men. There is no distinction in this respect. Can we feel surprise that their babes perish in the womb, or as soon as they have seen the light? The question ought to come home to the conscience of this enlightened nation, could it be expected that females, treated thus, anywhere in the world, should be mothers—should bear children, and not bury them!

The advocate of the system, may find a salvo for his conscience, and frame a falsehood with his lips, by saying, in palliation of his guilt, that the African mother has no natural affection for her own offspring. But this would be only to place the blame at the door of the Great Creator Himself. If she is destitute of natural affection, it is because it has been crushed out of her heart by oppression; for it is a natural instinct with which God has endowed all females for their young, for the preservation of the species.

The Parliament of England, after long years, aroused by the appeals of some of her philanthropic statesmen, saw the horrors of the system and abolished it, in her West India colonies. Would it not have been a glorious thing if these United States had been included, for the moment, in the number of her colonies? At least, we should have been spared the horrors of this fratricidal war!

And now I ask, have I not established the charge, stated near the commencement of this chapter, viz.: that the principal cause of the rapid decrease of the slave-population, in all countries where slavery has existed in its rigors, was owing to the fact, that their infant children have been sacrificed annually, by tens of thousands, on the altar of the slave-god? True, the tyrants did not order them to be strangled, at their birth. True, they were not, under the influence of pagan superstition, cast into the Ganges, or some other sacred stream, to feed the hungry crocodile. But, sacrificed under a system not less cruel and revolting than that ancient system of Paganism, their miniature graves are scattered, by hundreds of thousands, along the margins of the Mississippi, the Arkansas, the Brazos, and other streams now become as sacred as the Ganges. A great monument will be erected over those graves. At all events, a page will be written in history showing that their slaughter was avenged by the armies of the Republic, employed and commissioned as God's destroying angel, in the destruction of the First-born of the oppressors!

If there be a future life, how will these latter, confront the myriads of souls thus wronged and cheated out of existence? O, is there not a cry that has been going up to Heaven from those millions of little graves, scattered all over the South, against the nation that permitted this system of wrong! Can we wonder that the hour of atonement has come! God is Just! "Great and marvellous are thy works; just and true are thy ways, thou King of Saints!"

XII.

ENSLAVEMENT OF THE MIND.

SLAVE-HOLDERS have ofeen protested against the charge, which stands at the head of this chapter. But all their protests and arguments can avail nothing, so long as stubborn facts confront them, which remain unanswered.

It would indeed be difficult, nay, impossible to imagine a state of the total enslavement of the body, which should not'involve the enslavement of the soul or intellect. And all the arguments employed to prove the contrary, are utterly futile and void.

For one man to assert a claim of property— of absolute ownership in the very soul and intellect of another, is so revolting to universal reason, that even the stanchest advocate of slavery, stag- gers appalled at the thought of such treason against Heaven, and makes a feeble but ineffectual attempt, to repel the charge.

The system of slavery that has prevailed at the

South, debased the soul of man, and fettered the intellect, at the same time that it bound and fettered his limbs. To meet and obviate this objection, the more recent defenders of the system, have taken the milder position—that, of the right of property in the life-time service of the slave; whilst they disclaim the right of property in his soul, or his person. This, however, is a mere subterfuge, designed to remove from it, the odium inseparable from the idea of one man's holding his fellow-man as his property.

Let us look at the claim of the slave-holder, as stated in this milder form of expression. The Declaration of Independence, penned by the immortal Jefferson, asserts that " all men are created free and equal." It asserts, moreover, that all men were endowed with " certain inalienable rights, among which are life, liberty and the pursuit of happiness."

If this declaration is true, then the pursuit of happiness is one of the inalienable rights of all men. If the African is a man, the "pursuit of happiness" is a natural and " *inalienable right,*" which belongs to him as well as to all other men. If he is not a man, it devolves on the advocates of slavery, to prove that he is not.

But the slave-holder claims an absolute right of property in the life-time service of the slave. Now, the two rights, that of the master, and that of the slave, are irreconcilably in conflict, the one with the other. The one destroys the other.

For example, suppose that the inalienable right of the slave to the pursuit of happiness, should prompt him to put himself under a teacher, a few hours each day, for the purpose of being able to read the great and Blessed Volume of God's Truth, and of improving himself in knowledge generally; would not the master be compelled to relinquish his absolute right to the service of that slave, at least for the time thus daily spent by him in the pursuit of knowledge, and the improvement of his mind?

Or, suppose again, that, in the exercise of this "*inalienable right*" "the *pursuit of happiness*," the slave should express a desire to dwell with his own wife and family—If this right is acknowledged and maintained, what becomes of the master's right to sell him, or any of his family, thus separating them, perhaps, for life?

We see, therefore, that the right set up by the slave-holder, when expressed in its very mildest form, is totally opposed to the exercise of that "*inalienable right*, the pursuit of happiness," which Jefferson asserted, is the gift and birthright of *all men*.

We must, therefore, conclude, either that the African is not a man, or, that the statement in that memorable Declaration is not true, or, that the claim of the slave-holder is a fallacy. Which shall we conclude?

We cannot, certainly, conclude that the African is not a man, at least, till some advocate of slavery, bolder than his fellows, shall undertake seriously to prove that he is not a man. This, I believe, has never yet been done. And while they admit, without dissent, that the slave is a man, though with a dark skin, we may rest safe in the conclusion *that he is a man.*

In the next place, we may not, and further I say, we dare not conclude that the Author of our existence ever created any man without designing his happiness, and endowing him with an inalienable right to seek his happiness. This proposition is so clear that I have never known any slave-holder, or any advocate of the system to deny it. It is not only an inalienable right that belongs to all men, but is placed by Jefferson among the truths which are self-evident. To deny it, therefore, would be, in fact to insult the reason, and the enlightened conscience of universal mankind.

There is out one conclusion remaining, and that is, that the right of property to the life-long service of the slave, is a fallacy, having no foundation whatever in the eternal principles of right and rectitude ; since, as we have seen, this claim destroys the *inalienable right* of the slave to the pursuit of happiness, and is wholly in conflict with it.

But now, let us examine this pretended claim of the slave-holder. He claims the right—the absolute right of property in the service of his slave, as long as he lives ; but this claim, he argues, does not necessarily involve the enslavement of his soul, or his intellect. But this reasoning is self-contradictory and absurd,—let us see :

The services of a slave would be worthless to the master, without a sound and healthy body, able to render service. Besides, no service could be obtained from the sound and healthy body of the slave, without the consent and co-operation of the mind or soul, that controls all the motions and actions of his own body. It is vain to speak of separating the soul and body of a man, until death has effected a separation. They are so united, that they are a unit in this life, at least, and the body cannot act without the soul, nor the soul without the body. The master, who controls the body of his slave, in exacting service from him, does, so far control his soul, or his intellect. And he can exact no service from his slave, till the latter has first abandoned *all freedom of will*. His *will* must be so far brought into subjection to the will of the master, as to consent to be *governed by him*—to *will* what *he wills*—and to move all the muscles and limbs of his own body, as he, the master shall dictate. Is there no enslavement of the mind,—the soul in this? Can a more miserable and abject state of bondage be conceived of?

But let us see how the theory operates when carried out into practice.—The master has a cotton plantation, and it is his pleasure that the slave shall till and work that plantation, in the growth of cotton. Has the slave any freedom or liberty of choice? Though he should prefer some other employment—some other mode of life— though he should judge a life spent in a cotton field, and in clearing swamps, to be destructive of life and health, and subversive of all his hopes of pleasure and happiness in this world, has he any option? Must he not *bend his will*, however reluctantly, into *absolute submission* to the will of his lord? Yea, he must go, and sweat, and toil, and die at last, on the cotton farm, because the *master willed* it!

I might continue this chain of thought, almost indefinitely; but there is not space, nor do I find any necessity. There is, however, one phase, in this mental enthralment, which I must not, and will not omit to notice in this connection. I refer now to the *Legislation*, in most of the states and countries, where slavery has existed, for the express purpose of preventing the intellectual improvement of their slaves, and of keeping them down in a state of mental darkness and ignorance. This is a feature in African slavery, which, for blackness of guilt, finds no parallel in any ancient form of slavery the world has known.

If, to resolve that your slave shall be kept in ignorance—If, to enact laws for the purpose of keeping him in ignorance—And if, to exercise vigilance in the execution of those laws, does not involve the absolute and utter enslavement of the soul, then tell me what is meant by the enslavement of the mind of man, or how it would be possible to fetter and bind a human soul!

But has the God of the spirits of all flesh,

ever delegated authority to any human being, thus to impose shackles on the immortal mind, and to bind it down in chains of darkness?

Go, visit one of the large plantations, up the Red River, or the Arkansas, with a population of two or three hundred slaves. Search every hut, and you will not find a book, a pamphlet, or even a newspaper — not a single trace or sign of education in one of them. Not one of them can read a single letter in the book. There is no Holy Bible, no Testament, not even a religious tract in any of their dwellings. That plantation is, in fact, a dungeon of darkness, and its occupants are prisoners of darkness! The chains on their souls, have been rivetted by law! Now, if God has endowed man with intellectual faculties, for the purpose of being improved in obtaining the knowledge of Himself, through his works, and through his Word, who has the right to say to his fellow-man, that he shall not employ those faculties as God designed they should be employed?

Look again, on that plantation, and into that dungeon of darkness.—You will there see two or three hundred souls, with noble intellects, it is true, and faculties of a high order, such as God

endowed them with. But have those intellects
been expanded, and improved, and developed by
education? Have they been permitted to know
God, by the diligent study of his works and of
his Word? Have they had any chance or opportunity, to receive that mental culture and training, so essential to the highest happiness of man,
and which, we may say, was the end for which
every man was created?

Suppose I should ask the Christian master, do
you believe that your slave is a man?—that he
is endowed with intellectual faculties?—that he
has a soul? He would be compelled to answer
in the affirmative. Do you believe that the culture and improvement of those faculties, by education, is essential to the highest dignity and happiness of man? He would likewise be compelled
to answer, yea. And further, do you believe that,
when the Creator thus endowed man with such
noble powers, it was with the intention, that he
should exercise and improve those gifts, and
aspire to the highest dignity, and the highest
degree of happiness of which his nature is capable? Could he say, nay?

But what has slavery done? It has taken away
the key of knowledge—it has suppressed every

high and noble aspiration of the soul—it has, by legislative enactments, stationed armed sentinels at the gates of the temple of science, to prevent the slave-man from entering therein ; lest he should attain to that state of intellectual dignity and excellence, which is the ultimate end for which God created him, for His own glory!

Yea, this is the kind of legislation which has been tolerated in this Christian land—this land of boasted freedom, education, and equality! Surely, it was time that this state of things should have a termination. The end has come, but not in the way that we looked for! God's ways are not as our ways, nor his thoughts as our thoughts!

XIII.

BREEDING SLAVES FOR MARKET.

To assert that, during the last twenty years, two millions of slaves have been imported and sold in the sugar and cotton-growing States, from the more Northern Slave States, would be rather under than over a correct estimate. It may truly be said, that, the passion for buying negroes, amounted to a mania. It might be called the *Niggermania.* It was, in fact, a disease—And I have never known a disease, that was more contagious in its nature, or that prevailed to such an alarming extent. But there is nothing surprising in this circumstance, when it is known that almost every man's political and social standing in the community, was estimated by the number of slaves which he owned.

The planters of the South have acquired an unenviable reputation, as it is well known, for running headlong into debt. The reason of this was,

that every planter was willing, not only to ex-
pend his whole income, over and above the actual
expenses of his plantation, in the purchase of
slaves, but to buy as many more, in addition, as
he could obtain on credit. For example, if a
small planter, with a force of ten or twelve hands,
his cotton crop would probably net him (I speak
of the times just before the war) about five thousand dollars, of which sum, the actual cash expense of his plantation, if he were economical,
would not be over fifteen hundred dollars. The
balance he would be sure to lay out in the purchase of negroes. Thirty-five hundred dollars
would, in those times, now past and gone to return not again, purchase three or four likely
negroes. But, in addition, he would be sure to
purchase two or three more, on credit, relying on
the proceeds of the next crop, to make the pay-
ment. Thus, every thing they could make, was
expended in the purchase of negroes. The majority of them, even lived poor, and stinted themselves and their families, in many of the com-
forts of life, that they might have the more money
to buy negroes. And still they were always in
debt for the purchase of negroes. They raised
cotton, and they raised sugar, but only as a

means to enable them to buy negroes—more negroes. They never could buy enough of them.

To meet this great and ever increasing demand
for negroes, there was not a town, of any size, and
hardly a village, in any of these states, where
there was not a slave-mart, open day and night,
at all seasons of the year. At these marts, scores
and hundreds of men, women, and children of all
colors, from a jet black, to the lightest complexion,
that could hardly be distinguished from the fairest
circassian, were kept constantly on hand, for sale.
Almost every day, gentlemen, from the city and
country, and sometimes from other states, visited
these markets for the purpose of examining the
stock of animals for sale, with a view to purchase.
Not unfrequently, old bachelor planters and merchants visited these marts, *to purchase a wife or a
mistress*, provided they could find one to please
them. Every one, who is at all familiar with the
working of the system, is aware, that, some of the
most beautiful women, and young girls, have been
thus exposed to sale, at these numerous marts, and
for the purpose designated ; many of whom, on
account of their light complexion, could scarcely
have been distinguished from the white creole girls
of Louisiana, but for the clear, dark, and lustrous

eye, denoting the taint of African blood in their veins.

Out of this state of things, an important traffic grew up, denominated the *domestic slave-trade.* In carrying on this traffic, negro-traders were the merchants. Owing to the great and increasing demand for slave-property, this traffic soon attained to a high degree of importance.. A numerous class of men applied themselves diligently to the business for years, as their sole occupation, and none made fortunes more rapidly than they. Not a few of them became millionaires. I have in my mind now, one who thus acquired a property of nearly two millions, and then when he was fifty, married one of the most beautiful and accomplished young ladies in Tennessee, the daughter of a clergyman; which shows that the character of a negro-trader, was not held in quite so much odium at the South, as in other, *perhaps, less civilized districts.*

The greater number of the slaves, thus transported, from year to year, from one to another distant State, and sold to new masters, were furnished by Virginia, and the two Carolinas. Maryland, Kentucky and Missouri each furnished a few, but not the tithe of what were furnished by the first three named, which may therefore, without any injustice, be termed *slave-breeding-States*.

Much of the land in those States had become almost valueless, from long tillage by slave labor. This is one of the effects of slavery. The soil itself seems to experience the curse. The land gradually wears out in a few years, and becomes utterly worthless. The traveler, journeying through any of those older States, may often see extensive fields turned out, as waste and barren lands, so naked and bare of soil, and so exhausted, that not even weeds will grow on them.

There is many a planter in South Carolina and Georgia, who does not make over one or two bales of cotton to the hand, on account of the exhausted state of the soil; whereas, if he were in Mississippi or Texas, he could raise ten or twelve bales per hand. Slave property was, therefore, becoming almost valueless, for agricultural purposes, in several of the States; and the owners of slaves had either to emigrate to some new State, or turn their attention to some new enterprise. The Domestic Slave Trade sprung up just at the favorable juncture, to meet this necessity. And many of those who did not choose to emigrate to the newer States, taking their slave property with them, at once entered on this new and lucrative business of breeding slaves for market.

The great State of Virginia stands first and uppermost, in the list of slave-breeding States— Virginia, a name become venerable with sacred memories, as the mother of Presidents,—as the birth-place of Washington, Jefferson, and other eminent statesmen and orators, the noblest benefactors of the country. What a stain upon the bright record that might have been hers! How severely has the scourge of God come down on her soil, for her iniquity!

One of the wisest and most profound European statesmen of modern times, expressed his opinion of the practice of breeding slaves for sale, in the following strong and characteristic language: "The breeding of slaves for sale is, probably, the most immoral and debasing practice ever known in the world. It is a crime of the most hideous kind, and if there were no other crime committed by the Americans, this alone would place the advocates and supporters of American slavery, in the lowest grade of criminals."

Thus wrote Daniel O'Connell, the great Irish patriot, *par excellence*, a man of a towering intellect, and commanding genius, whose very name adds lustre to his country. He was in a position where he could view slavery from a stand-point, uninfluenced by self-interest and the prejudices of education; and, therefore, his opinion outweighs all that Southern writers and Southern divines have said and written on the other side.

It is not to be denied that this horrid practice has caused our whole nation to be despised by the civilized world. Another foreign writer, M. Cochin, a Frenchman, uses the following language in reference to the practice of breeding slaves, for sale: "What shall we say of that abominable fact,—negro-raising? It is well known that, among horses and cows, a fine stallion suffices for a drove. Some slave-holders have, in the same manner, one sire to several mothers; and the methods for raising the bovine and equine races are now brought into use for the human race, on the soil of liberty."

Such charges made against a great and Christian nation, by some of the most enlightened foreigners and journalists, cannot be answered by a witticism or a contemptuous sneer. There is so much of truth and justice in the charges preferred, that, unfortunately, we cannot vindicate the honor of the nation, against those who make them.

Some of the best families, in the older slave-states, revel in all the luxuries of wealth and affluence, from the profits *derived from slave-breeding!* They keep the young and healthy breeding women, and men enough to suffice for the purpose of sires, and sell the rest to the traders, who constantly traverse those states to buy up that species of property, with a view to transport them to another market. The process is very like that of the farmers in Kentucky and Tennessee, who raise mules and horses, to be sold in the states further South. The practice must strike every reflecting mind, on the very first blush, as revolting to every dictate of humanity, as demoralizing, in its effects, both on the slave and white populations, and as a crime against God.

To speak only of its effect, in sundering the ties of consanguinity, as the last writer quoted, truly says: "the husband is thus wrested, from his wife, the mother from her infant, the aged father from his son! This montrous, daily, inevitable consequence, the separation of the family, is, in itself alone, to every man of heart, the condemnation beyond appeal of slavery. Ah! our

hearts are rent with the thought that death may
suddenly snatch us from our wife or child!
What would it. be, if it were necessary, every
morning, to ask, is my child sold? Has my wife
been carried away? The stories of Mrs. Stowe,
are only the skillful and touching delineations of
these separations, the threat of which, always suspended, weighs on all the joys of the unhappy
negro."

XIV.

THE MARRIAGE ALTAR THROWN DOWN.

THE marriage relationship was originally established by God. There is no diversity of views on this subject, at least, in the christian world, whatever differences of opinion may exist in regard to slavery.

The union that, exists between husband and wife, was ordained in the beginning, by the Great Author of our being, and is, therefore, to all intents and purposes, a sacred and indissoluble relationship. All doubts on this point, if there could be any, is taken away by that inspired and authoritative declaration, " whom God hath joined together, let not man put asunder."

The intimacy and closeness of this relationship, is expressed, in that original ordinance, when marriage was instituted, contained in the 2nd. Chapter of Genesis, "Therefore, shall a man leave his father and his mother, and cleave unto his wife, and they twain shall be one flesh."

The law of marriage is palpably written in the
physical constitution of man, and in the deep-felt
necessities of his nature. In the same connection
where it is written, "God created man in his own
image, in the image of God, created he him "—
we find it also written ; "*male and female created
he them.*"

In all ages of the church, the saints have regarded the marriage institution as of divine appointment, and the obligations, growing out of it,
as possessing a sacred and religious character.
"*Let the same be she that thou hast appointed for
thy servant Isaac.*" This was the prayer of the
venerable and pious servant of Abraham, whom
he had made ruler over all that he had, when he
was sent to obtain, from among Abraham's kin-
dred, a wife for his son Isaac. This is explicit
testimony as to what was the opinion held by the
saints of patriarchal times.

Though this divine law of marriage, like every
other law of God, has been violated, and corrupt-
ed, and trampled down in many ways, yet, it
is wonderful to observe how a mysterious and
special Providence has been exercised, in every
age and country, to maintain and perpetuate that
law. For it has not been blotted out. It could

not be, without the destruction of man's physical and social being.   He was originally created "*male and female.*"   They are born into the world "*male and female*" still.   The man cannot do without the woman, nor the woman without the man.

There is an exact equality of the sexes born. This is a curious physiological fact, in the history of the race.   We know of no physical necessity in the constitution of man, by which this general result should be secured.   It is certain, that, while in some families, all the births are males, in others again, all the births are females.   And we can assign no reason or necessary cause, why it might not happen that all the births in a whole nation, should be, either all males, or all females, as well as in individual families.   But, if such a contingency should ever happen, the existence of that nation would, of course, be suddenly terminated.   Or, if in any nation or country, the sexes were born in disproportionate numbers—if, for example, in Utah Territory, or any other kingdom or territory, only a fourth part of the births were males, and the other three-fourths were females, we should conclude that it was the Will of the Divine Being, that polygamy should prevail in that kingdom or country, inasmuch as nature had provided only one husband for three women.   But, as there is born, in every kingdom and country throughout the whole world, just an equal number of males and females, we are impressed with the belief, that there is a Special and Overruling Providence, which has maintained and preserved this remarkable equality between the sexes, thus securing to every man his wife, and to every woman her husband, and making the original creation of *male and female*, a *perpetual* and *ever renewed* creation.

So much for the divinity and sacred character of the marriage relationship.   It is, further, essential to human felicity.   The cup of man's earthly bliss would lose one-half its sweetness, if this ingredient were wanting.   Even the joy of Eden was not perfect, till God had formed a help-meet for man.   The Creator saw, and he said, that, "it *is not good* that the man should be *alone*." And we may suppose, that, when Adam awaked out of his sleep to find a female form, of angelic loveliness, as a bosom companion nestling by his side, he felt that the measure of his happiness was complete.

In the present state of the world, the pilgrimage of man on earth, would be sad and dreary indeed, were it not that sin has not entirely thrown down the marriage altar, nor made utterly desolate the family circle. Universal as are the ruins of the fall, and as much as the beauty of creation has been marred by sin, there is still something of domestic bliss left to man. The purest, and the most unalloyed pleasure which has come down from Eden, is that which is found in the union between two congenial hearts, whom God has formed for each other, and which have been united together, in a life-long destiny. The world, may seem cold and cheerless—adversity may be his lot—but still the man who is thus blest, may find a ray of comfort around his own family altar, in the society of the sympathetic and loving being, whom God has given him to double the joys of life, and divide its sorrows.

African slavery is in direct opposition to this law of Heaven. It has *thrown down the marriage altar!* It has introduced a system of promiscuous concubinage, and wide spread fornication in the place of it, in all the States where it has prevailed.

I am aware, that the upholders of the system

manifest some sensitiveness under this charge. But they scarcely undertake to make any self-defense against it. The most they attempt, is, to retort on those who make the charge, by pointing to the lax state of morals in the Free States; as if the crimes of individuals, in any country, could be offered in extenuation of a legalized system of iniquity, on the part of a whole State.

The domestic slave-trade, which has been sanctioned and legalized in most of the Southern States, resulted, as it might have been foreseen, in a state of concubinage and whoredom so general, and I may even say, *so popular*, that custom has established it as a peculiar system of the South, as much so as slavery itself! For I do not believe that there is any other civilized country, at least, where the female is not looked upon as a degraded and fallen creature, who has lost her virtue. But there is no colored woman in the Slave-States, who thinks less of herself, or is less esteemed by others, because of the want of female virtue. But, on the contrary, if she is the mistress of a white man, she thinks herself elevated by the connection, and is envied by her female friends. Nor is the fine and polished gentleman of the South, who keeps his colored mistress, degraded in the eyes of his acquaintances, either male or female, nor his name cast out. It is notorious, that we once had a Vice President, from the South, who kept his colored mistress— but that circumstance did not injure his popularity at home.

Let me not be considered as a defamer of Southern institutions. I speak concerning a state of things which I know to exist. For the purpose of corroborating my testimony, I will here quote an extract from the writings of Chancellor Harper, whose testimony will be received as unquestionable; for he was a Southern gentleman, a native of South Carolina, and one of their ablest defenders of slavery. He says:

"She is not less a useful member of society, than before. If shame be attached to her conduct, it is such shame as would, elsewhere, be regarded as a venial impropriety—She has not impaired her means of support, nor materially impaired her character, or lowered her station in society; for she has done no great injury to herself, or any other human being. Her offspring is not a burden, but an acquisition to her owner; her support is provided for, and he is brought up to usefulness; if the fruit of intercourse with a free man,

his condition is, perhaps, raised somewhat above
that of his mother. Under these circumstances,
with imperfect knowledge, tempted by the stron-
gest of human passions, unrestrained by the mo-
tives which operate to restrain, but which are so
often found insufficient to restrain the conduct of
females elsewhere, can it be a matter of surprise,
that she should so often yield to the temptation?
Is not the evil less in itself, and in reference to
society—much less in the sight of God and man?
As was said of theft, the want of chastity, which,
among females of other countries, is sometimes
vice, sometimes crime—among the free of our own,
much more aggravated—among slaves, hardly deserves a harsher term than that of weakness."

Here, we have a shameless and unblushing
apology for this almost universal and even popular
system of prostitution, among the slave population of these States, by one of the most distinguished writers of South Carolina, and a firm
defender of slavery. He admits that the female
slave, who has parted with her chastity, has but,
at most, committed a "*venial impropriety*," which
hardly deserves a harsher term than that of
"weakness"—that she has not injured "*herself nor
any other human being*"—that she has "not ma-

terially impaired her character, nor lowered her station in society"—that her offspring is "an acquisition to her owner," who will be provided for, and if the fruit of intercourse with a free man, his condition will be raised "somewhat above that of his mother," &c. The facts are all just as the writer admits—And this is the state of public sentiment, and the state of morals that exists, and that has existed throughout the South. But, that which may well excite our astonishment, is the fact, that there should be found, even at the South, an intelligent and educated gentleman, willing to justify this state of things.

But it cannot be helped. It is a condition *inseparable from slavery.* It has been forced upon the enslaved and helpless population, and they have not the power to resist it. The laws of slavery, and the laws of the States that legalize it, have forced it upon them.

In the first place, they have done this by legalizing the *Domestic Slave-Trade*, whereby the rights and obligations of the marriage relationship are annulled, and husbands are forcibly separated from their wives, and wives from their husbands. See how the system works in a Slave-breeding State, where, on many a plantation, may be found, perhaps twenty or thirty young and healthy slave women, kept to breed and raise children for the market—but in all probability, there are not over five or six slave men on the same plantation. It would be out of the question for the master who follows slave-breeding, to afford a husband for each woman. And, of course, it would be impossible for each woman to have a husband. Is not the marriage altar thrown down? Is it rational to suppose that the enslaved, kept in ignorance under such a system, should be able to recognize the sacredness of the obligations growing out of the institution?

The traffic in slaves, in the second place, has annulled the ordinance of God, by taking away from the slave, the only incentive existing, that could induce him to assume the obligations imposed by that ordinance. He may be separated from his wife, the very next day after marriage, and so may the slave-woman be separated from her husband, never to meet again. They are liable to be sold and separated, at any moment. And would they be disposed to enter into such sacred relationships—would they form such endearing and tender ties,—only to experience the pain of having them sundered again, so suddenly and ruthlessly? There is no people on earth, who would do it, under the same circumstances. The marriage altar would necessarily fall into disrepute. But *the crime belongs to Slavery.*

Another way, in which slavery has impaired the obligations of the marriage relationship at the South, is, in the facilities it has afforded to corrupt men, for indulging their unbridled passions. A licentious planter, or overseer, might buy a mistress, at any time. She must go to his home. She is his property.— She is unprotected, and entirely in his power. —She has not the disposal of her own body or person. The fact is, it was just as easy to have a *harem* on a large Southern plantation, or even in a city like New Orleans or Charleston, as to have one in Turkey, provided the old rake of a planter or merchant, took a fancy to have two or three, or more beautiful and bright-eyed mulattos, about his bachelor establishment. Indeed, it might be said that, as a general rule, the female part of the population on a plantation, constituted the harem of the overseer. For no one would dare to resist his importunity. And that, as a general thing, the overseers at the South, did take advantage of their situation, and make "*acquisitions*" to their employers, is apparent from the many *living proofs*, which may be seen on almost every plantation.

Need any thing more be added, to set forth the horrors of slavery? In utterly casting down the marriage altar, it made war upon one of the institutions of Heaven, and that, too, the one in which nearly all the heart-felt sympathies and endearments of life, which this world affords, were concentrated.

Christian philanthropists will have a work before them, when this war is over, and slavery shall have passed away, in restoring that altar to its primeval place, and in erecting the standard of a pure morality among the slave population. This will be a work of time. It cannot be accomplished in a day. The social habits and sentiments of a numerous population cannot be suddenly changed. But this desirable reformation can be effected, by a proper effort, in a very few years. For there is not a more docile people on the face of the earth, than the colored race, nor one, apparently, more willing and even anxious to make improvement, in all that pertains to their spiritual and moral welfare. It is to be hoped, that this wide field for missionary enterprise, now thrown open, may be speedily and thoroughly occupied.

XV

THE PROCLAMATION.

THERE has been no Presidential term of four years, since this nation became a Republic, that will be so distinguished in future history, by great and memorable events, as the first four years of Mr. Lincoln's Presidential Supremacy. But the *great act* of his life, will be that, in which he subscribed his name to the document which loosed the chains of slavery, and gave liberty to millions who were held in bondage. That act not only gave freedom to four millions of the enslaved children of Africa, but it cleared away from the escutcheon of our nation's proud fame, the only dark spot that had rested upon it, and assigned, at once, to the great Republic, that position in the fore-front of nations, to which it was justly entitled, and which will be maintained, under the guidance and smiles of a propitious Providence, through all the coming years. That great hindrance to our national prosperity having been removed, we may expect the country from this date, not only to advance in a career of uninterrupted prosperity, but to have the distinguished honor of being the pioneer nation in the cause of freedom and humanity, to all other nations. She could not fairly, lay claim to this enviable distinction, which, nevertheless, fate had willed to her, while so many of her people were held in a state of bondage. Now, she can assert her claim, and now, go forward, without let or hindrance, in the fulfillment of her grand mission.

From this day, the soil of America, is a soil consecrated to freedom. A soil baptized, again and again, with the blood of the free, should be the home of the free, and the free alone. No more, O! no more, let the turf once reddened by freedom's costly offering, be pressed by the foot of a slave! Never more, in this land, now and forever redeemed, let the cry of a slave be heard, as he looks forth from the cell of his captivity, and utters his fruitless sighs for freedom! Countrymen of Washington! Descendents of the pilgrims! let us, without a dissenting voice, approach our country's altar, and there record our vows that we will be true and loyal to freedom's cause!

The first day of January, 1863, will be celebrated by posterity, as the day when the sun of America, first shone forth with an unclouded splendor. That sun arose amid the storms of the Revolutionary struggle—but it arose behind a dark and portentous cloud. The whole political heavens have been overcast and darkened by that cloud, threatening, ever and anon, to burst in a storm of destructive wrath over the whole land. It did burst at last, and descend in a flood of desolating vengeance. But, God be praised! the country is safe once more—the heavens have been purified—the threatening and portentous cloud has passed away, and the sun of our freedom begins to shine forth, with a full-orbed glory, shedding an effulgence that shall radiate and lighten distant lands.

So far as human instrumentality is entitled to any honor, for doing what God decreed should be done, in reference to the *Act of Emancipation*, that honor must redound to the name of President Abraham Lincoln—a name, now rendered immortal, and which will stand second only to that of Washington. His hand it was that laid the cap-stone in the completion of our Temple of Freedom. The foundations of that glorious structure, were laid by our fathers, under the guidance of Washington, but we must say, they left it in an unfinished state. It is true, they saw and they proclaimed the great truth, which none others had ever seen or proclaimed before them, that "all men are created free and equal," but still, they permitted some to continue in a state of bondage, and the work which they commenced, was left unfinished! It was scarcely possible that so perfect and magnificent a structnre, should be the work of a single generation. They gave us the theory and the constitution of a free government, almost perfect—with only a single defect. That defect is now removed, and we stand before the world, an example of the wisdom of the theory, announced by them.

We are wont to believe, that, when a great revolution or change is to be wrought, vitally connected with the destiny and happiness of whole nations, suitable agents and instruments are specially raised up to accomplish the work. Thus, we believe that our Washington was raised up, and that he was guided and sustained by a Special Providence, to fulfill the purpose of that Providence, in laying the foundations of this Empire of Freedom.

In the same manner, we must believe that President Lincoln was the man designated and raised up by the same protecting and overruling Power, to conduct this Nation through the gloomiest period of her history. There has not been a darker day in our National history, than the day when he took the helm of State. We thought the *Union* was irrecoverably gone! The ablest and wisest statesmen, both North and South, had exhausted all their efforts and counsels, at compromise and conciliation, but to no purpose. A cloud of gloom and despondency, seemed to cover all faces. But there was one man who did not despair of the Union, and whose mind was made up—and that was the President.

He summoned the Governors of the States together for consultation. He spoke:

"Gentlemen, the machinery of the nation is out of order. We must run it as we find it. Its intelligent wheels, its rods, its belts are separated, but the boiler seems to be perfect. We must repair the work, with such skill and ingenuity as we possess. There is wisdom in counsel, and, therefore I have called you, that we may reason together. What shall we do, that we may crush this foul rebellion, and preserve the country from wreck? I have made up my mind, with implicit confidence in an Overruling Providence, to meet all emergencies that may arise. It is time to work. What shall I do about issuing a procla- mation to the people?"

Here was firmness of purpose, and decision of character, which showed that the right man stood at the wheel, in the Pilot-house. Had he wavered then, and vacillated between hope and fear, as if he knew not whether to move forward or back- ward, the country would have been lost. Had he possessed the weak and cowering will of his predecessor, nothing could have saved the State.

The Governors seemed undecided, hardly know- ing what counsel to give. They were noble, brave, patriotic men, but even they seemed fearful, and appalled at that solemn crisis, when the nation's destiny trembled in the balance. After some mo- ments, during which a profound silence reigned, the President addressed Gov. Curtin personally— "What will Pennsylvania do, if I issue my proc- lamation?" There was another deep and solemn pause. But at length, the Governor, as if he had caught inspiration from the President, having read the firm resolve which flashed from his eye, and the confidence and hope which inspired his whole manner, energetically and nobly answered—"Sir, if you will issue your proclamation, Pennsylvania *will furnish you a hundred thousand men, in a week.*" The President grasped the hand of the Governor convulsively, and ejaculated "*thank God for that noble reply*—I will, at once, issue my proclamation." And he did issue it.

The "*nick of time*," that comes in the affairs of nations, had now come, and was past—The crisis was past, and the nation was saved from that hour. It is said that the President of the great American Nation, shed tears of joy, which mingled with those that suffused the cheeks of the patriot Governor of the Key-stone State. The gloom that enshrouded that conclave of men, passed away like the morning mist before the power of the summer sun; hope revived their drooping spirits, and joy took the place of sorrow.

Never, since this nation sprung into existence, has there been a man placed in so responsible and critical a position, as President Lincoln at that very nick of time. And never was there a man who met the crisis and the responsibility, with a more manly and becoming spirit. If he has political enemies now, we have no fear that posterity will not do him justice. His name will descend to history, as the *Second Saviour* of his country. But even if he had done nothing else during his presidential term, the *Act of Emancipation*, alone, would insure immortality to his memory.

It were greatly to be wished, that, it could be recorded by the impartial historian, that the Act of Emancipation, which gave freedom to four millions of human beings, who had been cruelly oppressed, had been a measure demanded by the united voice of the people, as an act of justice and humanity—and that the proclamation had been issued in answer to that demand. We may suppose that Heaven would have looked down, with a smile of complacency, at beholding the deed, and would have blessed our land!

But that proclamation was issued on the ground of MILITARY NECESSITY. We were *made willing* to open the doors of the prisoner, and to let the oppressed go free, because the measure was necessary *to save ourselves*, and to maintain the government. We regret that we are compelled to indulge the reflection that if *our own salvation* had not imperatively required the measure, the poor African slave might still have hugged his chains, and still have sighed in vain for freedom, under the very shadow of the temple of freedom !

We have, as a nation, done what was right, but not because it was right. We have performed a great and glorious act of justice, but not because it was justice. We have freed the slave from his abject and degrading state of bondage, but not because prompted by sentiments of pity and humanity. But, nevertheless, since the act of Justice, and right, and humanity has been passed, and there is an end of slavery, we will say that we are satisfied—that we are thankful !

The African people, will remember the house of their bondage, from which they were redeemed, with so many signs and terrible judgments. They will not forget the day, when they were proclaimed free. The first day of January will be *their great anniversary*, the annual return of which, will be celebrated by joyful acclamations and hymns of praise from a grateful people, down to the latest times. And while they give to the Great Creator, all the glory of their deliverance and their salvation, they will cherish the name of Abraham Lincoln, who was the chosen instrument in His hand, in accomplishing their deliverance.

XVI.

HOW TO DISPOSE OF THE LIBERATED SLAVES.

"TAKE no thought for the morrow, for the morrow shall take thought for the things of itself," is a wise and judicious saying, which may be commended, as worthy of attention, to that numerous class of philanthropists, who manifest so much concern about the future of the emancipated slave. One would almost conclude, from the unusual anxiety which they seem to feel lest these poor Africans should be *starved to death* among us, or be unable to find a home in this broad land, that they had been appointed as the guardians of the colored race, and were solely responsible for their future welfare, and their good conduct.

Now, it may be sufficient to remind all such charitably disposed persons, that they may consider themselves as relieved from all such responsibility, as the Divine Being is, "*de natura rerum,*" the Guardian of the race. He took care of them, when they were in bondage—He brought them out of a state of Slavery—And he can provide for them in a state of freedom.

If we did not know that it is written, "The poor are God's heritage," and that it is His special prerogative to take care of His own, we might believe these whining and sickly sentimentalists were in earnest, and meant something, when they utter so much *cant*, as to the future starvation and wretchedness in store for the Africans, as *the consequence of their emancipation.*

Of one thing we may rest well assured, and that is, the burden of caring for, and providing for their temporal support, will not fall on the Northern States. The South will be their future home, both because it is their native land, and the clime congenial to their nature. The apprehension that a tide of emigration will begin to flow towards the North, by which every town and county in the Northern States, will be overrun and burdened by hordes of vagrant and idle negroes, is altogether an imaginary evil, which, if it should happen, would be in direct contravention of all the known laws of nature.

The Africans are a gregarious or clannish people,

as much so as the Germans, the Irish, the Japanese, or any other distinct nationality or race. They prefer the society of their own people, when they can find it. The free blacks scattered through the Canadas and in the free States, are those, who escaped thither, at least the majority, to avoid oppression in the South. But when slavery is abolished, and when they can live in the South, and enjoy the rights and privileges of freemen, instead of there being a rush of this population to the North, the tide of emigration will set the other way, and many of those who had been shivering with cold, and freezing at the North, will be glad to seek their own congenial and native clime. Of course, from a variety of accidental and contingent causes, there will always be individuals of this race, as of every other race, scattered over the world. But I do not think, that, in ten or twenty years hence, when the new social order, consequent on this rebellion, shall be settled on a sure basis, there will be a larger proportion of the colored population in the Northern States, than at present. The great body of them will be massed together in the States bordering on the Gulf.

As for the idea of colonizing so many millions—

it is a utopian scheme. In reference to the necessity or utility of the plan, we might ask, *cui bono?*
Has the scheme ever been found practicable?
The States of South America emancipated their
slaves—Mexico emancipated her slaves. And
many of the Northern States emancipated their
slaves, years ago. But, in no instance was coloni-
zation attempted, nor, that I am aware of, even
thought desirable.

What evil has ever resulted from the fact
that they were permitted to remain in the States
where they were born? There have never been
any collisions between them and the white population. They have never betrayed a spirit of insubordination to the laws of the country. And,
I believe, that the first case of insurrection,
against those by whom they were liberated, has
yet to be recorded. Under all circumstances, as
their history shows, they have evinced a spirit of
forbearance, patience, and uncomplaining meek-
ness, such as no other people have ever exhib-
ited. Now, wherefore should a whole nation be
transported, at incredible expense, from the homes
of their birth, to another and distant continent?
The idea is absurd. It cannot be done—It will
not be done. There is no necessity, and no

reason in the world, why such a measure should be attempted.

Moreover, they can be made a useful population in this country. Indeed, their labor and services could not well be dispensed with. It would be like the amputation of a right arm, or severing a sinew that supports the body, for the nation voluntarily to deprive itself, of such an amount of useful and productive labor. A more egregious piece of folly could not well be conceived of. Rice, sugar, and cotton, are staple productions, and indispensable in all the markets of the world. And how are we going to do without them? The negroes are habituated to the culture of these staples. It is their occupation. And shall we deprive them of their occupation, and ourselves, at the same time, of these necessary and valuable productions, or become dependent on other countries for a supply of them?

Interest, then—the reciprocal interest of themselves and the white population, imperatively demands that they shall remain in the country, and apply themselves to the pursuits which they have so thoroughly learned, thereby gaining an honest livelihood for themselves, besides bringing a large revenue into the national treasury.

But will they not relapse into idleness and barbarism, after they are freed? The lying slander has been repeated a thousand times, by slave-holders, and the abettors of the system, that the negro will not work unless he is compelled by the lash ; and that the only way to keep him from running back into his original barbarism, is, to keep him in *Slavery.* I aver, after long observation, that *the only industrious* and laboring population in the Southern States, is the negro race. If there shall be any starvation, resulting from idleness, after the Act of Emancipation shall have gone into effect in all the States, it will not be among the once enslaved race, but among those who were formerly their masters. They never did work—They are not accustomed to it —They despised labor—They passed their days in indolence—And it will be no surprising thing, if many of them should come to want and beggary, or be supported by charity. It is to be hoped their *sympathizing friends* in the Northern States, will lend a gracious ear to their appeals, when they shall be made.

There never has been any substantial proof adduced, in support of the oft-repeated falsehood, that the negro-race are naturally more indolent than any other race, and that they will not work, unless compelled by the lash. A thorough investigation, in the West Indies, whence the slander was first started, has shown that they have never refused to work, when they obtained a reasonable compensation for their labor.

Let the officers of our army be called on, for testimony on this point, who have required their services at Vicksburg, and other places, in digging ditches and trenches, and in erecting fortifications. In all these Southern States, where the war has raged, they have been hewers of wood and drawers of water—in fact, they have been *drudges* and *slaves for our army*. But have they ever refused their services, when asked, in the first instance? Never! Whenever, and wherever it has been signified that work was required to be done by them, they have thrown themselves into it with an energy and good will, which ought to put to silence the lying calumny, at least, in the minds of all our military commanders.

The thousands of contrabands, who came into camp, when General Butler's army took possession of the Lafourch district, above New Orleans, were willing to return to work, every man and woman, upon the assurance that they were under the protection of our Government, and should not be left absolutely at the mercy of their former masters. And they have been working industriously ever since, for a bare nominal pay of two or three dollars per month.

No, it is not true, that the negro will not work. He has always been used to labor—And he has no aversion to it. And our Government could not commit a greater blunder, than to transport such a population out of the country.

But after all, there is an insuperable *prejudice* against the African race, in the minds of many, and they have got the idea, some how, into their heads, that the two races cannot, and ought not to dwell together, in the same country.

It is the merest folly to attempt seriously, to combat a weak and silly prejudice. But I would advise all those who have such a dislike to a dark skin, and to the peculiar odor of an African, as not to be willing to live in the same country, to emigrate to Europe, and leave America to the colored race, and to those who are willing to dwell on the same continent with them. In the Providence of God, they were brought to America, and it is just as much their country as it is that of the white man. And if there is a white man, who cannot live with the black man, let him leave the country, and return to the land of his fathers, and not demand that the black man be driven away, who has an equal right here with himself.

But there is no necessity—there is room enough in this country for all. Let those who have this peculiar dislike to the color of an African, remain in the Northern States. He will not often see an African there, to offend his sight, or his olfactory nerve. He is not compelled, by any necessity, to remove South, where the Africans will be principally congregated.

But now, seriously, I would ask, if the white and black populations could mix together, and associations, as to all the social relationships and duties of domestic life, were not so very disagreeable and irksome, when the latter were held in a state of slavery, what will render the same or similar associations so very repugnant and offensive, when they shall become intelligent and educated freemen? Some of the very élite of American Society, the aristocrats of the land, the educated, the fashionable, and the refined, have been able, not only to dwell with them in the same country, and to tolerate their dark color and their African odor, but they even had such a partiality and affection for them, that they could not do without their presence in the nursery, in the kitchen, in the parlor, and in every other department of domestic life. They could hardly relish their food, unless prepared by the hand of some negro cook. In short, the African was considered as an essential element in the constitution of *a perfect social system.* And we may conclude, that, there will be multitudes who will be able to abide still on this continent, although the negro-race should not be compelled to leave it.

Let them reman in the land of their birth. Let them continue to cultivate the fertile rice districts of South Carolina, and the lowlands of Florida, Louisiana, and the Mississippi and Gulf coasts, in sugar and cotton. We shall need these staples, and none can produce them so well as they. We can give them churches and schools. And Providence can work out the problem, that, the African can be developed into the highest type of man. It is the destiny, which, beyond a peradventure, awaits them. Another age may see, that, though the different families of man, are distinguished by certain peculiarities of language and climate, yet they are but *one family*, after all, and can dwell together in harmony and peace, in the same country, and under a common government. This is the *lesson* we ought to learn. That it is the design of the Great and Supreme Father, we should understand it. there can be no doubt.

XVII.

RELIGIOUS CHARACTER OF THE NEGRO.

THERE is one element in the native African character, which proves, at least, that they are endowed with immortal souls, and that is, the strong and original tendency, in their minds, to religious devotion. Materialistic writers have endeavored to create doubts, whether there be any such thing as *mind* or *spirit*, as distinct from man's corporeal being, and capable of an existence, separate from, and independent of the body.

I have never bestowed any thought on such writers, believing their speculations to be utterly unworthy of notice. If the creation of a man, proves the existence of an intelligent Creator, so does the creation of man as *a religious being*, prove the fact of his accountability—and if he is accountable to his God, he must be immortal, and the proof of this, is inscribed on his physical being,

by the finger of Jehovah, notwithstanding all that
infidels have said.

There is no other religious animal in the world,
that we know of, but man.   Man is, by his nature
and original constitution, a religious being.   And
if this proves him to be immortal, the argument
is conclusive to prove that Africans have souls.
I make this observation, on account of the many
puerile and ridiculous attempts to prove the inferiority of the negro race.   It is true, none of
them had the hardihood to avow that negroes
have not souls.   But the whole drift and tendency
of the speculations of some of them looked in that
direction, and indicated plainly enough, that, it
was just what they would have avowed, if they
had not feared the effect of such an avowal.

Dr. Samuel Cartwright styled the negro race,
the "*Prognathous race.*"   He says "the typical
negroes of adult age, are proved to belong to a
different species, from the man of Europe or Asia,
because the head and face are, anatomically, con-
structed more after the fashion of the Simiadiæ
(monkeys) and the brute creation, than the Cau-
casian and Mongolian species of mankind, their
mouth and jaws projecting beyond the forehead
containing the anterior lobes of the brain.   More-

over, their faces are, proportionally, larger than their crania, instead of smaller, as in the other two species of the genus man. Young monkeys and young negroes, however, are not prognathous, like their parents, but become so, as they grow older."

Here is another brief quotation from the same essay of the learned Doctor: "On another point, of much importance, there is no practical difference, between the Rev. Missionary (Mr. Bowen) and that clear-headed, bold and eccentric old Methodist, Dr. McFarlane. Both believe that the Bible can do ignorant, sensual savages no good; both believe that nothing but compulsatory power can restrain uncivilized barbarians from Polygamy, inebriety, and other sinful practices." This conclusion of the Doctor, if they are as near akin to the monkey tribes as to the genus man, is natural and legitimate.

The Baptist Missionary Bowen had been to Africa, sent thither by a society in Charleston. He had been brought up in Georgia, and all his prejudices were in favor of slavery. He found the natives of Africa in a condition so far inferior to that of the slaves of his own native State, that, he hastily, and I will add, wickedly concluded, that the only way to christianize the Africans was to enslave them.   Dr. Cartwright seizes the conclusion, but too well predisposed by his theory, and makes a bold and rash attack on the Bible, as an instrumentality, inadequate to the conversion or civilization of savages.   Adopting his theory and conclusions, we should never have attempted the conversion of the natives of the Sandwich Islands; but we ought to have sent pirate ships thither to bring them away in chains, and then to have sold them into slavery, before we attempted their conversion.   Nay more, we should first have enslaved the Cherokee and Choctaw Indians, resident in the Southern States, before we tried to christianize them.   We remember very distinctly, that, when the attempt was first undertaken, with the Bible to convert and civilize them, there were many who, like Dr. Cartwright, believed it could not be done.

It is to be lamented that such a writer should be able to quote the opinion of a Christian minister, in favor of the infidel sentiment.   It is not only a *slur* on the Bible; but it is an inversion of the order of things ordained by God, to say, that the Bible can do no good, till "*compulsatory power*," or slavery, has *restrained uncivilized bar-*

barians, from polygamy and other sinful practices. The Bible is God's great *moral lever,* to move the moral world—the *only lever* that has ever moved it, the only one that can move it. Nothing else has ever curbed and restrained the sinful passions of men, and produced morality in the world. The most reckless infidel would hardly presume to cite us, to any instance of a nation, with a pure system of morality, without the Bible.

I hazard the remark, that, if one quarter of the sum expended in fitting out ships during the last two or three centuries to rob Africa of her children, and in carrying on the Slave-Trade, had been expended in sending Bibles to Africa, and missionaries to instruct the natives to read it, there would not have been a barbarian, on the whole continent of Africa to-day.

They are just as religious by nature, if anything more so, than the Indian, or the native of the South Sea Islands. And, as to their intellectual character, if there is any difference between the African, and the Asiatic or the Indian, every capable and impartial observer will give it, without the least hesitation, in favor of the former. There is a certain sprightliness of character and genius, belonging to the negro, which does not belong to the Asiatic or the Indian.   Physically, he is altogether the superior man.

Having spent many years in ministerial labors, both among the white and black populations, at the South, I am prepared to express the opinion, that there is a far greater amount of genuine religious piety, among the latter than among the former.   The religious statistics of different communities would confirm this statement.   There are as many colored church members in the Protestant churches of New Orleans, as there are white communicants, although the white population is more than twice as great as the colored. Take the city of Richmond, and the same thing is true.   There are more colored than white communicants.   There is a single African Church in that city, numbering over two thousand members, which is more than the whole number of white communicants in all the churches, although there are two white inhabitants for every colored person in the city.   Could these things be so, if the negro were naturally, more depraved than other men, and insusceptible to religious and moral influences?   Do not such facts prove that Africans have, even more of the religious element in their nature, than the whites?

I would not assert, that, throughout the Southern States, these relative proportions in the numbers of the pious, would be kept up between the two populations. For very obvious reasons, there would be found to be considerable variations. And one principal reason is, that the two classes do not enjoy, and never have enjoyed the same or equal religious privileges. There is many a large district or region, where the slaves have no means of grace. I could name a single planter, who owns, at least, a thousand negroes, who, I suppose, would not give a dime to pay a minister of the Gospel to preach to them, to save them all from eternal perdition. For he is a wicked old sinner, and does not believe in the Gospel. Where they are denied the means of grace, it is not to be expected that they should become religious. But give them the same advantages with the whites, and I am strongly inclined to the belief that, everywhere, they will be the more Christian people. I offer no reason for this opinion, only, that so far as my observation has extended, *everywhere, it is so.*

I am aware that there are many, very refined and elegant people, who do not place a very high estimate on a negro's piety. They think

him a *superstitious* rather than a religious being,
and his piety is taken for superstition rather
than religion. I know that there is, generally,
a fervor that characterizes the religious devo-
tions of the African, not often to be found in
the worship of white congregations. But we cannot think the Father Supreme will deem their
humble sacrifice as less worthy of his notice, because their whole heart is in it. True, they may
not be permitted to worship in temples of gothic
structure, built by art, and richly decorated—
Their ministers may not be the most graceful
and polished in their manner, and may not be
able to round each sentence in their sermons, according to the most classical and elegant model
—And they may have no deep-toned organs to
accompany their loud and clear voices in hymn-
ing Jehovah's praises. But still, they generally
sing with a fervor and spirit, not always found
in our more fashionable congregations, where the
music is made, not by the worshippers, but by
hired substitutes.

I remember that, on one occasion, during the
year 1847, I heard the sublimest strains of church
music I ever listened to, in that grand African
church in Richmond. Indeed, I may say, I never

expect to hear such church music again, on this side of Jordan ; for really I know of no fitter words, to convey a proper idea of its effect on my mind at the time. The church edifice occupies the site of the old theater, that was burned some years ago. They have a large choir, who are instructed in the science of music. But, I can say that some of their voices sounded to me more melodious and musical than the sweetest-toned instruments. Church-organ music is nothing compared to it. It would be difficult to persuade me that the Africans cannot, as a general rule, sing better than the whites. But the most interesting feature in their music is, that, it always seems to come from the heart.

It is true, this may be all mere superstition, or religious enthusiasm. And I may be considered, by some, as tinctured with the same sort of enthusiasm myself, for the expression of such sentiments. But I cannot help it. I am bound to think that the Supreme Father must have a special regard to that people, who have so large a share of the *divine* or *religious* element in their natural character.

If there is any principle in a human being that may be called divine, it certainly is the *reli-*

gious element of his nature.   And we have a right
to conclude that the nation or people which have
this principle developed in the highest degree.
must have a high and noble destiny in reserve
for them.

Here, I must borrow one of Emerson's *carly-
lisms*, for it well expresses my meaning :

"I esteem- the occasion of this jubilee (West
Indian emancipation), to be the proud discovery
that the black race can contend with the white ;
that, in the great anthem which we call history,
a piece of many parts, and vast compass, after
playing a long time, a very low and subdued
accompaniment, they perceive the time arrived
when they can strike in with effect, and take a
master's part in the music.   The civility of the
world has reached that pitch, that their more
moral genius is becoming indispensable, and the
quality of this race is to be honored for itself.
For this, they have been preserved in sandy
deserts, in rice swamps, in kitchens and shoe-
shops, so long ; now let them emerge, clothed,
and in their own form."

XVIII.

THE COLORED REGIMENTS.

At a late hour, the Government has determined to call in the aid of the African, for the purpose of putting down this mighty Rebellion. After having tried, in vain, for two years, the experiment of subjugating the South, without permitting a single colored man to become a soldier, and even after having refused their services when voluntarily offered, in the common cause, they have at last been compelled, reluctantly, to arm the negro to save the Union!

If this policy had been adopted at the very beginning of the struggle, it would have been ended months agone. But a decree had gone forth, which no policy of man could counteract or circumvent, that the victims required as sacrifices on the bloody altar, in this war, must be of the white, not the black race. And the consequence is, that, we have offered up our own sons and brothers by the hundred thousand. To preservo our own soldiers from utter extirpation, and to preserve our National existénce, we have at last, *magnanimously*, consented to let tho negro bear an honorable part, in the effort to maintain the substance of Republican Liberty.

Tell me, in the name of reason, why it is that a great and enlightened people, in a war for liberty, and for the preservation of free institutions, has ignored the very existence, except as chattels and slaves, of an army of more than half a million of men, able-bodied, patriotic and brave, but as unfitted by the very fact of their deep oppression and enslavement, to takc any activo part in the struggle for freedom? There was a fatuity in it! There is no other answer.

It was not because they wcre lacking in patriotism, or attachment to the Union-cause—for that has never been doubted. It was not because they were deficient in physical courage, and could not fight as soldiers—for every intelligent person, who has any knowledge of the African character, knows the very reverse to be truc. The African is the best type of the physical man, in all Southern latitudes. Even the veriest advocate of slavery, who has always lived at the South, and

known the African character, has been willing to
concede to them the possession of physical courage. Chancellor Harper, one of their best au-
thorities, says :

" They are, by no means, wanting in physical
strength of nerve. They are excitable by praise,
and, directed by those, in whom they have confidence, would rush fearlessly and unquestioning,
upon any sort of danger. With white officers,
and accompanied with a strong white cavalry,
there are no troops in the world, from whom
there would be so little reason to apprehend
insubordination or mutiny." He further, adds :

"If, at any time, we should be engaged in hos-
tilities with our neighbors, and it were thought
advisable to send such an army abroad to
conquer settlements for themselves, the invaded
regions might have occasion to think, that, the
scourge of God was again let loose to afflict the
earth."

These sentences indicate, clearly, that this highly
educated Southern gentleman entertained no ordinary opinion of the physical bravery and capa-
cities of the negro race.

All who have read the accounts of the San
Domingo Revolution, must know something about

the fiery enthusiasm of the African in the tumult
of battle. The very same quality of his nature,
has, more than once, been proved, since this sanguinary contest was commenced. Colonel Higgin-
son, commanding the first regiment of colored
troops in South Carolina, as we remember, testi-
fied that he had never read nor heard of anything to equal the fierceness and fiery ardor of
their attacks, except in the history of the French
Zouaves. A similar record will go down to history, in honor of the Kansas Colored Regiment.
In a late battle in Arkansas, the commanding
General reported, that, they fought against three
times their number of Texans, for hours, with an
obstinacy never surpassed, and finally routed them.
Another battle-field, fought in the same State, near
Helena, where about one thousand of our troops
contended against more than twice that number
of the enemy, according to the reports published
at the time, was saved entirely by the valor of
the colored troops that belonged to the corps—
they were determined not to surrender—victory
or death was their watch-word—and, though some
of their white officers basely fled, they fought and
held the enemy, till reinforcements came to their
relief. Such records as these speak volumes.

In the Gulf Department, the African regiments have had no opportunity to test their fighting qualities.   They have been stationed at Forts Jackson, Pike, St. Philip, Ship Island and other places, to do garrison duty.   In June last, when there was a lack of men to press the siege at Port Hudson, and to make the contemplated assault, a portion of two or three of the regiments of Native Guards, (colored), were ordered to be transferred thither, and took a part in the bloodiest engagement fought during that siege.   They were ordered to take a certain battery, in possession of the enemy—they took it, though in doing so, some hundreds of their number fell, of the wounded and killed.   It was said, at the time, that they would have held the battery, if they had been sustained by the white troops—but, that, not being sustained, they were compelled to fall back from the position they had gained, under the concentrated fire and numbers of the enemy.   But they had proved their courage, and the commanding General thought it not improper, in an eloquent address, to pay them a deserved and just tribute, at the time, for the valor displayed by them.

It was in that assault, that Captain Kieux, of

the First Regiment, was killed. No braver man, ever lived. He was as black as the ace of spados. Yet he was an accomplished gentleman, and every officer who knew, loved and respected him. He was indeed worthy to be called a countryman of the brave and illustrious Toussant. I shall not soon forget his expressive countenance, and the impression made on me by his bland, and easy, and gentlemanly manners.

I will not say that our own soldiers have not fought well, and done their whole duty, on every battle-field; but, I must say, that, if any comparison is made between them and the black troops, as to the courage and other soldierly qualities of each respectively, the palm cannot yet be awarded to the former.

If Gen. Butler had organized fifteen or twenty of these regiments of black Native Guards, instead of three, only, in the fall of 1862, as he probably would have done, had he remained in that department, they would have been able, under the lead of officers only as brave as themselves, to march through western Louisiana, and into the very heart of Texas; and no force which the rebels had in the field, could have successfully opposed their progress. But, instead of carrying out the

policy, so wisely commenced, of arming the slave
population, the work was suspended for some
months, and the contrabands, fugitives from slavery, who came within our lines for protection
and liberty, were remanded back to the plantations, to work, many of them, for their old rebel
masters, for a nominal pay of two or three dollars per month, instead of being transformed into
freemen and soldiers of the Republic, as brave
and efficient as any the world ever saw.

Let no reader suppose that I indulge in exag-
gerated statements. Many of the best military
judges, who have visited the camps of the Louisiana Native Guards (colored), and seen them on
dress parade, have acknowledged them to be
fully equal to any other regiments. As for the
Second Regiment, stationed on Ship Island, I
can say, that, of the scores of officers, who have
visited that station, many of them fully prepos-
sessed against the blacks, and against the policy
of arming them, I have not known one who has
gone away without being made a sincere and
genuine convert to the system. Many of these
military gentlemen have expressed the opinion,
that this colored regiment is, in drill and discipline, in manly and robust form and appear-

ance, and all that constitutes an efficient military
corps, quite equal to any other regiment or corps
they ever saw on parade. Of course, this is saying much, but I am not giving my own opinion,
as I do not profess to be a critic in such matters; but I am giving the expressed opinion of
others, who are judges. But I can say, that, they
march better than any other soldiers I have ever
seen. They march to the music—with a step so
uniform and simultaneous, that, one would almost
be inclined to believe that the whole army moved
with one set of joints. No one can see a whole
regiment in motion, with their neat uniforms and
furbished arms, without a thrill of pleasure and
pride.

One reason, perhaps, why they appear to an
advantage, as compared even with some of our
white regiments, is, that they feel a sort of
ambition, and think there is something of glory
in belonging to the great Army of the Republic, battling for the cause of Freedom. They feel
that they have been elevated in the scale of humanity. And it is but natural that they should
desire to show themselves worthy of the honor
conferred on them, and the confidence reposed in
them.

The Africans, as a race, have more enthusiastic fervor in their nature, and are more governed by impulse and sympathy, than any other people with whom I am acquainted. It is for this reason, that, if we go into their religious assemblies, we always witness a display of far more earnest devotion and fervor, than is ever seen in our more phlegmatic and formal white assemblies. The same principle in their nature, would fire a whole army of them in the field of battle, and fill them with an enthusiasm which would render them invincible, and utterly reckless of danger. This is the true explanation of the fact, that, as proved in the wars of San Domingo, and wherever else their courage has been tested, they have been found *more daring,* if not better disciplined, than any other soldiers.

The negroes, not only have an *ardent* temperament, or *enthusiastic* nature, which is the very first and most essential element to make a good soldier, but here, in the South, they possess powers of *endurance,* beyond any other class of the inhabitants. This fact is so generally known and admitted, that no additional testimony can be needed on this point. Indeed, the learned Dr. Cartwright has asserted, in his writings, that it is impossible to work a negro beyond the point of his powers of endurance, so as to injure his constitution, or cause his death. The assertion is, upon the face of it, absurd and wholly untrue. But still, it is certain that their power of endurance, under exhausting fatigue and labor, is a marked feature in the character of the race.

It is not an easy matter to speak of the value of the aid, which Providence made accessible to us, and which we have rejected and despised, in the conduct of this murderous and destructive war. Was it necessary to spare the blood of the Africans in our midst, and to pour out our own? Did we set a higher value on the lives of the negroes, than we did on those of our brothers and sons? There was a fatuity in this, as before stated!

There was, what we may call a judicial blindness, which had happened to the nation, because it seemed to be necessary, as a condition of Justice, that the expiation for the guilt of the nation, should be made, not in the blood of *the guiltless*, but of *the guilty*. We shall see in the end, perhaps, that, of those who *had not sinned*, but *were sinned against*, not more victims will be offered on the red altar of war, than will barely suffice to teach us, of what service they might have been, if we had been wise enough to employ them.

We did not prosper in the war, so long as we let slavery alone, and resolved to spare it as a veneraole institution. For nearly two years, a series of bloody disasters and defeats attended our arms. But scarcely had our President uttered his solemn *threat* to the rebels, that unless within a specified time they laid down their arms, and returned to their allegiance, he would deprive them of their idol, the god which they had worshipped, when the victory of Antietam was announced, which sent a thrill of joy throughout the nation— as if the God of nations had even deigned to put the seal of his approval upon what was nothing more, in fact, than a simple *threat* or promise to do *right*—to do *justice*, in a certain contingency.

Well, the rebels would not lay down their arms, nor submit to the Government, and the President was necessitated to issue the threatened Proclamation. It was done reluctantly. And after all, it was but a partial act of emancipation, as it left many still in a state of bondage, whose chains might have been struck off, by the same blow, and at the same instant.

I would again repeat my most solemn conviction, that the war will be protracted, and we shall suffer, till we are thoroughly *corrected*, as a nation.

If we had, at this moment, and we might have had, a compact army of one hundred thousand of these Africans, well disciplined, and under brave leaders, they would subdue the rebellion. The South could not raise an army that would dare to face such a host of well-armed and impetuous negro-soldiers. I feel almost as sure of this as I do of my own existence. They would put an end to slavery every where, as they marched through the country, thus depriving the Rebellion of its main prop and pillar, and obtaining almost a bloodless victory. The people of the South, if thus threatened and invaded, would speedily come to terms and ask for quarter. For, that they could muster an army, consisting of the sons of planters, and others thoroughly acquainted with the ardent and fiery nature of the African, who could be induced to encounter such a host in hostile array, upon *equal terms*, is a thought that has never entered into my conceptions. And there is no intelligent person, who could, for a moment, entertain such an idea.

In the first place, their pride, and all their early

prejudices, and the notions instilled into them by education, would cause them to shrink from a contest, with an army of negroes, upon terms of equality. In the second place, they would know, what every one else must feel well assured of, that the army of negro soldiers would be able to *endure*, or to *hold out* in a fight, at least twice as long as themselves. And in the last place, they would have a conviction, that, in such a contest, fighting not only for *freedom*, but for their *very existence*, and armed by despair, such an army would have inscribed upon their banners, *victory or death*, and they could never hope to conquer them.

Thus, we see what *might* have been done. But I venture to predict, that, we shall not have such an army in the field, of these fiery, sable sons of Africa, until just about the period when the war is ended.

And then, we shall need their help, not to crush the rebellion, but to keep the rebels in subjection, after they have been subdued. The Government intends to put them in forts and garrisons, and other exposed places, for the purpose of guarding and securing the citadel of our freedom, after it shall have been re-established.

Thus, in the Providence of God, they are to be appointed to act as patrols or sentinels, to watch and keep down those, by whom they had been so long watched and kept down. They are to be *the masters*, in turn, where they had been the *slaves*. There is something like a stern but just retribution in this. *Fiat voluntas Dei.*

XIX.

THE AUTHOR'S EXPERIENCE AMONG THE REBELS.

My life, since I have been a man, acting on my own account, has been spent in the South, in the midst of Slavery. No sentiment or opinion, therefore, contained in the foregoing pages, has been received by me second-handed, but is the result of my own personal experience and observation. I know what I have written about. I know the people of the South, and their institutions, thoroughly. I have looked at slavery in all its phases.

I acknowledge that I never did believe slavery to be the very *summum bonum* of all human blessings. When I left Ohio, in 1831, and came South, and ever since I have been in the South, I have had but the one opinion in regard to slavery, and that is the opinion so often expressed by Jefferson, and other distinguished statesmen, that it is a violation of the natural rights of man, contrary to the letter and spirit of the sentiments contained in our Declaration of Independence, and opposed to that sense of *natural justice*, forming a part of the universal conscience of man, which is, therefore, rightly considered as an exponent of what is the Will of God, on the subject. I never did, I never could believe slavery to be right, in the abstract.

A sincere believer in the Bible, I have been looking forward to a better age, the promised Millennial age of the world, when, I firmly believed that slavery, and war, and every other form of evil, will have been purged out, and when, according to the promise, "there shall be nothing to hurt nor destroy, in God's holy mountain."

How this moral reformation of the world was to be brought about, it is not necessary now to inquire. But I believed it was to be done by *moral means*, and the circulation of the Bible, that great *moral lever*, which God has put into the hands of the Church. I was rather inclined to believe, that slavery, in this land, would come to an end, in the same way. But I have discovered, that, in this, I was mistaken. God had a controversy with our nation, which could not be settled in this way. There were past *wrongs* which could not thus be rectified and redressed. I see my mistake now. I see and own God's justice. As a nation, we had lost sight of this eternal principle, written in His Word, and inscribed on the very Heavens, "Justice and Judgment are *the habitation of Thy Throne.*"

I acknowledge that my first impressions of slavery, on coming South, were not of a kind to strengthen even if I had possessed any early prejudices in favor of the institution.

I passed the first year in Greene county, Alabama, and boarded in the family of a respectable planter, a member of the Baptist Church, and the owner of about twenty-five slaves. One circumstance that was novel to me, as I had never been accustomed to any thing of the kind, was, to be awakened every morning, or nearly every morning at day-break, by the sound of the overseer's lash. And as I knew that every stroke cut the skin and the flesh of the naked back of a slave, it made me feel *nervous*, before I had got *used to it.* This was the *morning bitters*, administered to each slave who had not performed a given task, or picked so many pounds of cotton the day previous.

I might have remonstrated with the master,

against the cruelty of the practice, but I was then a young man, and a stranger in the country, and I knew it would do no good, but might get myself into a serious difficulty. I have seen the same proprietor and master, on several occasions, use a raw-hide on the person of his house-servant, a delicate looking woman, about half white, and desist from the whipping, only when he was actually exhausted, and could indulge his wrath no longer. I remember, that, it occurred to me, on one occasion, to count how many more stripes he would inflict, after I supposed he had already inflicted, at least one hundred and fifty, and appeared almost exhausted with his effort, and I counted one hundred and fifty more, making fully three hundred stripes that poor woman received, at one time. Of course, there was no part of her body that was not marked, and her garment was so stained, that, it would have been difficult to say whether *crimson* or *purple* were not the original color. At first, she uttered loud and piercing cries—but these grew fainter and fainter, till, at last, they subsided into a low, moaning sound, hardly audible, as if she were engaged in a prayer,—but whether it was addressed to her master, or to her master's *Master*, I could not decide.

And yet, that man was a member of the church in good standing. Whether the victim of his wrath, was a member of the church with him or not, I cannot tell. He was an acting justice of the peace, at the time, and, in all respects, stood high in that community. I have no reason for thinking that he was more cruel to his slaves than other masters. So far from it, he was a humane and kind master as compared with many— perhaps, I may say, a majority of the slave-holders at the South. I am speaking of a state of things which I noticed, on first going South, and of what seemed to be the ordinary and established state of *discipline* for the slaves, in that community. No body appeared to suspect there was any moral wrong in inflicting one hundred, three hundred, or even five hundred stripes on the back of one's own slave, whenever he might take it into his head, thus to indulge his humor. For this was the common custom of the country, and there seemed to be no law against it. But, as it struck me at the time, the system appeared to be one of cruelty. And I am, now, more than ever established in the opinion, previously expressed in these pages, that, the system was not only founded in cruelty and blood, but, that it has been upheld by the same means, so that a righteous Jehovah could not tolerate its existence any longer in this land.

The following year I went to Mississippi, and boarded in a family where the regime observed in the government of the slaves, was about the same as in the family with whom I had lived in Alabama. However, I had an opportunity, while in this family, to learn something of the modes of torture, or their manner of dealing with runaway slaves, so as to cure them of that propensity.

The man who was to be punished, was a young man, apparently about twenty years of age, fully six feet in height, and a bright mulatto, nearly as white as myself—so near a white man, in fact, and so intelligent looking withal, that, I could not help feeling a strong sympathy for him, although I dared not to express it. He was staked to the ground, face downwards; and burning wisps of straw were passed over his naked back and loins, till he was covered with blisters. The pain, of course, was excruciating at the time, but not calculated, permanently, to injure or maim the slave. I record the circumstance, merely to show how ingenious is cruelty, in devising the means of inflicting torture and pain. I had read of many ways of torturing victims and criminals, but I had never read nor heard of this particular mode. But if I should proceed to relate all similar circumstances and facts that have come to my personal knowledge, directly or indirectly, I should have to write another book, instead of a short chapter, which it is not my intention to do, at present.

For several years, before the public sentiment of the South, growing out of slavery, culminated and broke out in the Rebellion, I had come to the conclusion, that, liberty in those States, was at an end.

The terms, *yankee*, and *abolitionist*, had come to mean nearly the same thing—and two more opprobrious epithets could hardly be conceived of, in the dialect of a Southerner. If a man happened to have been born at the North, he had to show very clean papers to avoid being branded as an abolitionist ; and with that brand once fixed upon him, there was no safety, any where in the country. He was liable to be hung up, without judge or jury, on any post-oak or black-jack, where he might happen to fall into the hands of a mob.

In the year 1860, I was residing in the State of Texas, in a village called Hempstead, fifty miles from Houston, on the railroad leading from that city to the northern limits of the State. In the month of November, before the State had as yet seceded, and before any vote had been taken on that question, our National flag had been dishonored, and trailed in the dust of the streets, by the rabble. As *secession* was the great topic of the day, and all classes of people were discussing it, some opposed, but the greater part in favor of it, I also, thinking myself a pretty good Southerner, ventured to have an opinion on the subject, and to express it, not dreaming of any danger or violence to myself, from doing so. I happened to remark, in a private conversation, that, if the South should secede from the Union, there would be war ; and that, in the event of a war between the North and the South, the institution of slavery would be overthrown. This I said, not from any unfriendly feeling to the South or to Slavery—but I intended it merely as an argument, why the South ought not to secede, but to adhere to the Union. I also further remarked, that in such a contest, the North would have every advantage over the South, as they had the navy, and in numerical force, were three times as strong as the South.

I should have remembered, that, in expressing these opinions, I was not a *slave-holder*, and, therefore, not one of the privileged class. I was waited on the next morning, while at breakfast, by five of the most prominent citizens of the town, who informed me, that, as it was understood, I had expressed opinions at variance with the views and feelings of the resident population, my presence was desired at a public meeting, which would be immediately convened.

I will confess that I felt some misgivings at first, knowing that hundreds of men had, during the past few months, fallen victims and been hung by the blood-thirsty and brutal mob of the State; and that I had myself narrowly escaped out of their hands only two months before—so narrowly indeed, that my name had actually been inserted among those who had been hung, in several newspapers of the state.

The meeting was called, at once, and there was some excitement. But I had several friends at that meeting, who knew that I was not an abolitionist. Fortunately, Colonel Wash. Crawford, an eloquent lawyer from the neighboring town of Washington, and the most influential man in four counties around, was there. He arose, and, unex-

pectedly by all, made such a speech in my defense,
as shamed even those who had accused me. He
had known me for several years, and my own
conscience acquitted me of the charge of abolition-
ism. If any body had called me an abolitionist
at that time, I should have considered it a gross
personal insult.

I was released, and, of course, I was free once
more, but not to express my opinions without reserve. I was taught, that, from that day, I must
observe caution. But I have, ever since, considered myself indebted to Colonel Crawford, for
my rescue out of the hands of a lawless rabble.

I did not feel safe, and could not breathe freely
in Texas, from that day ; and, although all the
interests I had in this world, lay in that State,
I began to think seriously of leaving it. As soon
as I could make the necessary arrangments, I did
leave, and found myself in New Orleans. in the
following April.

On the 12th of that month, the rebel batteries
were opened on Fort Sumter. I had, till then,
cherished the vain hope, that, somehow, or in some
way, the dreaded crisis might be avoided. But
now, all hope of the kind, was gone, and my mind
was decided. I was convinced that God had

made the Southern people mad, in order that they might bring ruin and judgment on themselves, and I said in my heart—Amen—So let it be—since they will have it so.   There is no reflecting mind in the country, but must accord in the sentiment of General Hamilton, expressed in one of his late speeches—"*The veriest skeptic, one who never before believed in a God, cannot 'but recognize in this war, the hand of the Almighty.   Slavery has been permitted to perform its mission, and its career is ended.*"

As I was necessarily detained, for several months, in New Orleans, endeavoring to transact, through an agent, some unsettled business in Texas, I again, suddenly and unexpectedly found myself *in limbo*.   I was summoned before his honor, Mayor John T. Monroe, to answer to the charge of having expressed *Union sentiments*.   The informants against me were Messrs. Smith and Rucker, certain horse traders, who had been stopping a few days at the same boarding-house with myself.   The substance of their complaint against me was, that I had said, I was for the Union. In this, however, they falsified, for they had never heard me make use of any such remark.   I had endeavored to be guarded in my words.   It was however, perhaps, a fair inference from remarks I had made use of, in a casual conversation with one of them.

In speaking of the state of affairs in Missouri, I did incidentally remark that the majority of the people in the State, ought to rule—and that Gov. Jackson ought to be governed by the action of the Convention, which was the only medium, through which, the voice of the people could be heard. He dissented from the view expressed by me, and the next day I had a citation to appear before the Mayor, to answer for my words. I had never had the slightest personal altercation or difficulty with either of the above named accusers. I had never wronged them, and I can think of no motive which could have actuated them, thus, *voluntarily* and *gratuitously*, to become my accusers, only their *hostility* to the Union. I have not been able to learn what became of Smith, as I lay in durance vile for nine months. But I do know that Rucker, several months prior to the arrival of General Butler to the city, went, on a cattle speculation, into Texas. He had obtained the cattle, a very large herd, and he would have made a fortune by the speculation, for beef was then selling in the city for twenty-five to fifty-cents per pound. But unluckily for him, the cattle were on the coast, above the city, just as Admiral Farragutt passed up with his victorious fleet, and he captured the whole drove. Rucker afterwards appealed to General Butler, and whether by taking the oath, or by some other process I cannot say, obtained damages to the amount of some hundred-thousand dollars, less or more. As he is still in the city of New Orleans, enjoying his *otium cum dignitate*, I trust this matter will be more thoroughly sifted, as it can be reduced to a demonstration that he was a thorough rebel, and that he intended the cattle for the Confederates, and not for the Federal Army.

The Mayor turned me over to the care and guardianship of Harry Mitchell, keeper of the City *Work House*, who had acquired such distinction as a recruiting officer for the rebel army, that even Russell, of the London *Times*, heard of his fame, and had to pay him a compliment in his journal, while on his visit to the city. He says: "The New Orleans papers are facetious over their new mode of securing unanimity, and highly laud what they call the course of instruction in the humane institution for the amelioration of the condition of Northern barbarians, and aboli-

tion fanatics, presided over by Professor Henry
Mitchell, who, in other words, is the jailer of
the Work House Reformatory."

That *course of instruction*, over which the papers
were so *facetious*, was usually not very long, but
it was most thorough. I should suppose that
the Professor sent not less than a thousand men
into the rebel army. I will not dwell on the
means employed by him to get soldiers to enlist,
but will give a single case, which may serve to
convey some general idea.

Three Irishmen had been brought into the
Work House, at one time. They said that they
had been arrested, for no other offense, only that
they had refused to enlist as soldiers in the
Confederate Army. Whether they stated the
truth or not, as to the cause of their arrest
and incarceration, it is certain, that, on the
very next day after, they were called on by
Professor Mitchell, with a recruiting officer, and
asked, whether they would enlist, on condition
of being released from the Work House, which
all three of them promptly declined to do. The
Professor and the recruiting officer went away;
but, the day after, those three men were loaded
with irons, and set at work breaking rock, with

heavy sledges. A negro, *perhaps*, might stand it to break rock all day long, in the hot sun, with a twenty pound sledge, and irons weighing sixty or seventy pounds chafing his ancles, but no Irishman can stand it, and, at the end of the first day, the three men signified their willingness to *enlist* in the rebel army ; and accordingly, the Professor turned them over to the recruiting officer.

Perhaps, I might not have given the Professor a notice, so much more extended *than* Mr. Russell thought it necessary to bestow on him, but for the fact, that, I am under greater obligations than Mr. Russell for personal attentions received from the Professor. And besides, as he still presides over the same " *humane institution*," under the auspices of the *Federal* Government, it is no more than simple justice to let the public know, that he is a faithful servant to those who employ him, at one hundred and fifty dollars per month, with the perquisites of office, amounting to as much more.

I cannot speak of what I suffered in that Work-House. I could wish that the nine months of cruel penance there for Liberty's and conscience' sake, could be blotted from my memory. Involuntarily, sometimes, as thought recurs to that dark period, I find my hand pressing my forehead, as if I would press back the thought, and relieve myself of such melancholy recollections.

How varied are the scenes of this life! What a world of tribulation we live in! There may be those who receive their portion of good things here; but the christian should ever bear in mind, that, if he would wear the crown at last, he must first learn to endure the cross—according to the saying of one of the best saints that ever lived,— "*no cross, no crown.*"

XX.

CONCLUSION.—THREE PARTIES.

THE stern and inflexible justice of Jehovah, in superintending and directing the affairs of political States and kingdoms, is the great and practical lesson, which we have learned from this war. Slavery was a great evil—just as great as has been represented, and as has been proved, by facts which cannot be controverted—but it was not too great an evil for the Genius of Christianity to conquer and destroy. It was a system that must have crumbled and disappeared gradually, before the moral power of truth and righteousness, as the Gospel gained sway. It would be a stigma upon our Divine system of religion, to say, that there is not a moral energy in the Gospel, adequate to the final overthrow of slavery. To deny to Christianity the possession of this moral power, would be a concession to infidelity, which we are not willing to make. It is the power, by which, the complete moral renovation of the world is to be effected, and the consummation of the Millennial age to be achieved.

Christianity has, more than once, demonstrated its power, to grapple with and vanquish the monster, *Slavery*, with the weapons of spiritual, instead of carnal and bloody warfare. For, it was nothing else but the voice of Christianity, as has been before insisted, speaking through some of her noblest sons, which led to the suppression of the African Slave Trade, and the emancipation of the slaves in the British West Indies, *without blood.* With multiplied proofs of this kind, as to the power of the Gospel, it would betray the most inexcusable ignorance, or something worse, to assert that the redemption of our own land from the curse of slavery, might not have been effected in the same peaceful and bloodless manner.

But there was an insurmountable barrier in the way, and that was the law of Jehovah's Throne, requiring that *National crimes shall be corrected by National judgments.* So much innocent blood had been shed, that, an atonement, *by blood*, had become indispensable, to vindicate the justice of the Divine Law. Here was Justice arrayed against Mercy, in a case, where it was necessary that the latter should yield to the former. Many good men and statesmen, besides Mr. Jefferson, predicted, long ago, that the claims of justice would yet be vindicated, against the slave-tyranny.

The Secessionists of the South, or the Pro-Slavery party, are *directly* responsible for the war, and all its consequences.

The radical Abolition party, in the Free States, must have the credit, by their agitation of the subject of slavery, and their violent and offensive manner of conducting the controversy, of having alienated the Southern people, and driven them to that suicidal act, by which they rushed on their own destruction. The collision between these two parties, led to the awful tragedy, of which this great land is, at present, the theater. If there had been no Abolitionists, there would have been no Secessionists, and, of course, no civil war. But now, since the consummation has been reached, we have no fault to find with the means, since it was brought about, in the *Divine Purpose*, to scourge and correct the nation.

It would be unjust, however, not to discriminate

between this radical Abolition party, and the true, loyal Anti-slavery party of the country, who, indeed, constitute the mass of the intelligent and honest citizens. This loyal, Anti-slavery party —that was the Conservative party before the rebellion—had no part, and no instrumentality whatever, in the horrible deed of initiating the war. They endeavored to prevent it. They were always in favor of conciliation and compromise; and, if their counsels had prevailed, there would have been no war.

President Lincoln is, to-day, at the head of that party, and he represents them; but he is not an abolitionist. Secretary Chase is another noble and patriotic representative of the same party. And we may say of nearly every great and leading mind in the country, who has anything to do with the Government or the Army, that they belong to this loyal, Anti-slavery party. It was the party to which Washington once belonged, and Jefferson, and the Adamses, and Madison, and Benjamin Franklin, and Alexander Hamilton, and the peerless Webster, and the eloquent Henry Clay. For every one of them believed slavery to be an evil, and deplored its existence. But it would be an insult to the memory of any of them to say, that they were Abolitionists, of the Wendell Philips and Garrison school.

And can we believe—would it be possible to persuade us, that, with the whole moral power and spirit of Christianity, in opposition to slavery, and the sentiments of all these great statesmen and philanthropists, whether now living, or dead, arrayed against the horrible system, it could have prolonged its existence beyond the close of the present century, if the Abolitionists had not sprung up, and interfered with the work which they had begun, of bringing about a reformation by mild and peaceful measures which are so much more in harmony with the laws of Divine Charity? But I reiterate what has been already remarked, that, crimes of such a nature had been committed against the rights of humanity, in the name of Liberty, that Heaven must have suspended its ordinary laws, not to have exacted a terrible retribution from this Nation. Hence the Abolitionists had a mission to perform.

The party has been in existence over thirty years, and what have they accomplished in that time? They did not convince slave-holders of their error, but, rather drove them, in self-defense, to adopt the *divine-right* principle in favor of slavery—a principle which, never before, had been asserted. They did not lighten the oppression of the slave, but rivetted tighter the chains of his bondage, as thousands who have lived at the South could readily testify. And finally, to them belongs the honor of having been employed as the instruments to bring this war upon the country, to the end that it might be purged and redeemed.

In speaking of the Radical Abolition party, I would be understood as referring to those, only, who advocated the "Malum in se" theory. This was the *New Gospel,* which caused the *division* of churches, founded under the preaching of the Old Gospel, and which existed together, in harmony and love for ages. It was this *New Gospel* which taught slaves to *run away* from their masters; whereas, the Gospel preached by Paul had taught them to be "*obedient*" to their masters, and even to "endure grief, suffering wrongfully." This *New Gospel* taught slaves, that, in effecting their escape from bondage, they might *steal* whatever articles they should consider necessary, to speed them in their flight to a land of freedom; which was contrary to the Moral law contained in the table of the ten commandments, which *forbids theft.* This *New Gospel* required its expounders and advocates, to apply such kind and fraternal epithets, as *man stealers kidnappers, thieves*, etc., to all their Southern brethren involved in the evil of slavery; which was contrary to the Gospel of Christ, who, 'when reviled, reviled not again, nor returned railing for railing." In fine, this *New Gospel*, openly, inculcated treason against the Government, by denouncing the Union as a *curse*, a *compact with hell*, etc.; and by disallowing, for years past, its leading defenders either to vote. or have anything else to do with a Government so corrupt. It is certain that if they had had the power, they would have destroyed the present Government and dissolved the Union, thirty years ago. Their work is at length accomplished, and now their mission ends.

But I do not intend by this to say that they have accomplished the destruction of the Union, although some of them have said, and are still saying that they *don't want the old Union*. I trust that old Union will be as lasting and firm as the mountains and hills of the great continent, over which it stretches. We would not acknowledge the mighty struggle in which we have been engaged, to maintain that old and glorious Union, formed by the wisdom and cemented by the blood of our ancestors, a failure, by saying that we shall have a new and better Union. A better Union it may be, but not a new one. If there was any dross, with that which before was gold, and that dross is separated or consumed by the fire through which we are passing, that is not to say that the gold itself is consumed. If there was a dangerous cancer or sore on the old body politic, and that sore has been probed and cut away by the scalpel which the war has applied to it, that is not to say that the body itself has been destroyed.

Let us not dishonor the memory of the great and good men who were specially raised up, for the purpose of forming the best Government ever yet enjoyed by any nation, under which we have so long lived and prospered, by saying that the work which they accomplished is a failure, and we must organize a *new government!* Shall we give up that grand old Republican form of Government which Washington and his compeers bequeathed to us? Never! Never!! If, from time to time, any defect or imperfection is found to exist, it may be remedied. If, in the Union itself, any weakness is discovered, even that may be remedied. This civil war will make the Union stronger than it ever was before. There may be fewer States, or more after the war, but it will be the same Union. There were but thirteen States when that Union was formed, but many States have been added to it since. Yet we do not say there is a new Union formed, every time a new State comes into it. It is the same old Union. Even so, if any State should drop out of the Union, it would not thereby be destroyed; it would be the same Union still.

It is a suggestive fact, that the loyal Anti-slavery party—it was the Conservative party before the war—we would call it the Constitutional party— some call it the Republican party,—and certainly, no one who is a Republican, ought to object to the *name*—but whatever name it may be known by, it is the party to whom that gracious Providence which has ever watched over the destiny of the nation, has specially entrusted the maintenance of the Union, and the preservation of the Government, in the terrible and fiery ordeal through which we are passing. The two parties, the Pro-slavery and radical-Abolition—which sought to destroy the Union and brought the war upon the country, have been left out—Providence seems to allow them no part in administering the Government in the present crisis. It is a suggestive fact.

There is another party, which occupies rather an anomalous position at present—which can hardly be said to be a party, but a fragment of the old Democratic party—the *Peace-party*—the *Copperhead-party*—who live in the Free States, but whose sympathies and hearts are with the rebels at the South—who are in favor of a reconstruction of the Union, with the institution of slavery intact—and this too, when they must see and know, that the horrors of slavery have reached their climax in the perpetration of the blackest treason against both Heaven and earth, ever yet committed by devils and wicked men! This *Peace-party* should not live in the Free States, but they ought to take up their abode among their secession friends at the South, where they properly belong. They may struggle on a little longer, as a drowning man catching at straws, to keep from sinking ; but it will be a vain struggle. The power of the party for good or for evil, is at an end.

The loyal Anti-slavery or Constitutional party, have ever been as much opposed, in sentiment, to slavery, as the radical Abolitionists themselves, and have ever believed that it was an evil of such a nature, as must necessarily come to an end, in the progress of events. But they were not willing to scatter firebrands, arrows and death, and to involve their country in the conflagration of a civil war, in order to destroy an Institution which they had no hand in creating. They were willing that the people in the States where it existed, and that Wise Providence over them, that controls and disposes, finally, of all such questions, should have the entire management of an affair, that had been placed beyond their own control. And now, when the people of those states have appealed to arms, and the Lord has permitted the *madness*, to seal the doom of Slavery, what could we do, but accept the issue forced upon us? The time for conciliation and compromise expired, when this issue was joined. It is vain to talk of Conservatism now.

It is, perhaps, worthy of notice, how guarded and cautious our President has been, in striking down slavery, not to trample under foot at the same time, the Constitution which he was sworn to observe. While the Pro-slavery party have anathematized him for interfering with the Institution at all, the radical Abolitionists have vilified and denounced him for not striking a more effective blow. They would have had him emancipate the slaves in the *Loyal* as *well as in the disloyal* States ; when they know he had no power to do so under the Constitution. It was only the *War-power* which gave him the right to emancipate the slaves of rebels—but it gave him no right to interfere with slavery in the loyal States. He has pursued a wise and prudent course ; and every loyal man in the country must honor and respect him for having confined himself, strictly, within the limits of Constitutional authority. When slavery is dead in the rebel states, it will soon die a natural death, in the loyal districts where it has been left remaining. Public sentiment at the South against the Institution, from present indications, will soon be so potent, and, almost overwhelming, that no man who thinks any thing of his own honor, will be willing to be known as a slave-holder, and they will voluntarily emancipate their slaves. The few who might be unwilling to do this, will find how utterly vain will be the attempt to hold their slaves still in bondage, when the slaves all around have obtained their freedom. It would be contrary to the instincts of humanity, to suppose that these millions of emancipated slaves, who have just begun to taste the sweets of liberty, would feel no sympathy for their brethren still held in bondage, and make no efforts for their liberation. Yes, slavery is dead—the temple of the huge and decrepit old idol is demolished. The wheels of his bloody car had crushed more victims into the earth, than ever did that of Juggernaut. But, I venture to predict, that, in ten years more, our American soil, thrice hallowed and consecrated with blood, will not be pressed by the foot of a single slave.

And to whom will the honor of this victory be due? To the Pro-slavery party? Just as much due to them as to the radical Abolitionists. They made the war, and the war has destroyed Slavery. But they did not aim at this result?—they made the war to maintain and perpetuate slavery. Will the honor be due to the radical Abolition party? The party has ever been very small and insignificant. They have never had control of the National Government. They did not send forth the proclamation of freedom to the slaves—and they have never brought liberty to a single slave, except perhaps to a few scores, whom they may have aided to run away from their masters. If their leaders could have succeeded in their designs they would have dissolved the Union long ago, and erected two Republics out of the old one, viz : a free and a slave-Re-Republic ; separated from one another only by Mason's and Dixon's line, but giving to the latter the richest and fairest portion of the American Continent, over which to extend and propagate the curse of slavery, perhaps for centuries to come. No, a Wise Providence has conferred on the loyal, Anti-slavery party, the honor of terminating the existence of this evil in our land. President Lincoln, acting as executioner, held the axe in his hand, by which the head of the old Dagon was severed from his body.

In conclusion, the christian reader will not fail to see most palpable proofs of the guidance and leadings of that Wise Providence, in all the re-markable vicissitudes through which, as a people, we have been made to pass. It was not because the Lord abhorred us as a people, but because of his great favor towards us, that he hath purged us, as gold is purified in a furnace. We have a great mission to perform, and there is a bright destiny before us, in the future ; and it was necessary that we should receive a discipline to prepare us for both. It was designed that we should be not only a great, but an upright people.

Who can doubt, that, when this war is over we shall be a greater and a more liberty-loving people than ever before? Our mission is to give to the nations of the earth, a practical demonstration of the great problem, never before solved, that, *man is capable of self government.* It is to be our destiny, to teach all tyrants and oppressors, that their days are numbered. We are to be a city set on a hill, whose light cannot be hid. With what fond anticipations, and earnest, kindling hopes, the eyes of millions, are, at this moment, turned towards this land! We should be recreant to the trust committed to us by our Heavenly King, if we should disappoint them. But He will not permit us. I have come to believe, that, He has guarded and brought us on so far, He has us under his special guardianship.

We know that all earthly blessings are prized, according to their cost. Why is it that the people of this country, value liberty and a free Government, beyond all other possessions, except that they are the children of those, who passed the ordeal of a seven years' bloody war, under the most trying and painful circumstances, in order to obtain that boon? If that war had had no other effect, than to generate in the whole American heart, an invincible and undying love for freedom, it were an inheritance well worth all the cost.

So, if we have been chastised with another three years' war, on account of *Slavery;* if we have been humbled to the dust, and made to drink our own tears, for having connived at oppression, under our free government; and, if we have been compelled to loosen the fetters of every slave, after having sacrificed hundreds of thousands of our brave sons and brothers, what else can we expect, but, that it will serve still to strengthen our attachment to the cause of liberty and free government? Is it probable that, hereafter, we shall have any sympathies on the side of tyranny, in any of its forms? All the discipline and training we have had, as a nationality, in the school of past experience, are of a nature to make us the devoted and perpetual friends of freedom. We have been educated and brought up in the school of independence. The words of the "Declaration of Independence," with us, will have a meaning, hereafter. There will be found neither knaves nor fools, who will attempt to fritter and explain away their significant import, as has so often been done, in the past. We have pretty thoroughly and practically learned the lesson of freedom, which it was the intention of the Divine Teacher that we should understand.

I repeat my most sincere and honest conviction, that, it is not for naught, our nation, as yet comparatively in its infancy, and far from having attained its manhood, has been so violently rocked in the cradle of Liberty. We have a mission to perform. Onward then, my grand, noble, free country! God speed thee onward, to the achievement of the wonderful destiny before thee! Methinks, I see in thy extended horizon, on every side, the dawning of a glorious morning.

FINIS.

www.ingramcontent.com/pod-product-compliance
Lightning Source LLC
Chambersburg PA
CBHW030730280326
41926CB00086B/1039